MACMILLAN MODE

Macmillan Modern Dramatists
Series Editors: *Bruce King* and *Adele King*

Published titles

Further titles are in preparation

MACMILLAN MODERN DRAMATISTS

ANTON CHEKHOV

Laurence Senelick

Professor of Drama,
Tufts University

MACMILLAN

First published 1985

Published by
Higher and Further Education Division
MACMILLAN PUBLISHERS LTD
Houndmills, Basingstoke, Hampshire RG21 2XS
and London
Companies and representatives
throughout the world

Typeset by
Wessex Typesetters Ltd
Frome, Somerset

Printed in Hong Kong

British Library Cataloguing in Publication Data
Senelick, Laurence
Anton Chekhov.—(Macmillan modern dramatists)
1. Chekhov, A.P.—Dramatic works
I. Title
891.72′3   PG3458.Z9D7

ISBN 0-333-30881-6
ISBN 0-333-30882-4 Pbk

To the memory of James Arnott

Contents

Contents

List of Plates

List of Plates

A Note on Translations

All translations from Russian are my own, except where otherwise noted.

LS

Editors' Preface

The *Macmillan Modern Dramatists* is an international series of introductions to major and significant nineteenth and twentieth century dramatists, movements and new forms of drama in Europe, Great Britain, America and new nations such as Nigeria and Trinidad. Besides new studies of great and influential dramatists of the past, the series includes volumes on contemporary authors, recent trends in the theatre and on many dramatists, such as writers of farce, who have created theatre 'classics' while being neglected by literary criticism. The volumes in the series devoted to individual dramatists include a biography, a survey of the plays, and detailed analysis of the most significant plays, along with discussion, where relevant, of the political, social, historical and theatrical context. The authors of the volumes, who are involved with theatre as playwrights, directors, actors, teachers and critics, are concerned with the plays as theatre and discuss such matters as performance, character interpretation and staging, along with themes and contexts.

BRUCE KING
ADELE KING

1
A Life

Nature and life conform to the very same outdated stereotypes that even editors turn down. *Chekhov to Suvorin (30 May 1888)*

Anton Pavlovich Chekhov was born in the town of Taganrog on the sea of Azov in southern Russia on 17 January 1860[1], the third of six children, five boys and a girl. He might have been born a serf, as his father Pavel Yegorovich had, for the Emancipation came only in 1861; but his grandfather, a capable and energetic estate overseer named Yegor Chekh, had prospered so well that in 1841 he had purchased his freedom along with his family's. The boy's mother Yevgeniya was the orphaned daughter of a cloth merchant and a subservient spouse to her despotic husband. To their children, she imparted a sensibility he lacked: Chekhov would later say, somewhat unfairly, that they inherited their talent from their father and their soul from their mother.[2]

The talent was displayed in church. Beyond running a small grocery store where his sons served long hours, – 'In

1

my childhood, there was no childhood,' Anton was to report[3] – Pavel Chekhov had a taste for the outward trappings of religion. This was satisfied by unfailing observance of the rites of the Eastern Orthodox Church, daily family worship, and, especially, religious music. He enrolled his sons in a choir which he founded and conducted; and aspired to be a pillar of the Taganrog community.

Taganrog, its once-prosperous port, now silted up and neglected, had a population that exceeded fifty thousand during Chekhov's boyhood. Its residents included wealthy Greek families and other Europeans, the ship-building interests. The town benefited from such public amenities of the Tsarist civic system as a pretentious-looking *gymnasium*, which the Chekhov boys attended, for one of Pavel's aims was to procure his children the level of education needed for entry into the professions. The upward mobility in the Chekhov generations is reflected in the character of Lopakhin in *The Cherry Orchard*, a self-made millionaire whose grandfather and father were serfs on the estate he manages to buy. Chekhov's father, born a serf, had risen from *meshchanin* or petty bourgeois[4] to be a member of a merchant guild; and Chekhov himself, as a professional physician and writer, became influential on the national scene. He was a model of the *raznochinets* or person of no settled rank who had begun to dominate Russian society in the latter half of the nineteenth century.

To bar mass advancement, the tsarist curriculum laid great stress on Latin and Greek; one recalls the schoolmaster Kulygin in *Three Sisters* chuckling over the fate of a friend who missed promotion because he could not master the *ut consecutivum* construction. Schoolmasters are usually portrayed by Chekhov as narrow, obsequious and deadly to the imagination, no doubt the result of his own experience as he studied the classics, German, Russian and, for a brief time, French. His best subject was Scripture. School days were lightened by the fairy tales of his nanny, the picaresque reminiscences of his mother, vacations spent on the estate his grandfather managed, fishing, swimming, and, later, visits to the theatre.

As a boy, Chekhov was stage-struck. Although it was against school regulations, he and his classmates frequented the gallery, often in false whiskers and dark glasses. Besides attending the active and not inelegant Taganrog Playhouse, Chekhov was the star performer in domestic theatricals, playing comic roles like the Mayor in Gogol's *Inspector General* and the scribe Chuprun in the Ukrainian folk opera *The Military Magician*. While still at school, he wrote a drama, called *Without Patrimony*, and a vaudeville, *The Hen Has Good Reason for Clucking*. Later, while a medical student, he tried to revise them, even as he completed another farce, *The Cleanshaven Secretary and the Pistol*, which his younger brother Mikhail recalled as being very funny. It concerned the editing of a sleasy newspaper and featured a double-bed as the major set-piece. Never submitted to the censorship, it is now lost.

By 1876 Pavel Chekhov had so mismanaged his business that, fearing imprisonment for debt, he stole off to the next town, to take the train to Moscow. There his two elder sons were pursuing their studies. He had already stopped paying his dues to the merchant guild and had reverted to the status of *meshchanin*. Whether Anton suffered a psychic trauma at this loss of caste, as had the young Ibsen when *his* father went bankrupt, is matter for speculation; certainly the repercussions felt at the sale of the home left their trace on many of his plays. Dispossessed of house and furniture, his mother and the three youngest children also departed for Moscow, abandoning him in a home now owned by a friend of his father. He had to support himself by tutoring

3

for the three years needed to complete his course. He did not rejoin his family until Easter 1877, his fare paid by his university student brother Aleksandr; and this first visit to Moscow and its theatres set standards by which he henceforth judged the quality of life in the provinces. Suddenly, Taganrog began to look narrow and philistine.

Just before Anton Chekhov left Taganrog for good, a public library opened. This enabled him to read classics such as *Don Quixote* and *Hamlet*, a work he was to cite indefatigably, and, like any Victorian schoolboy, *Uncle Tom's Cabin* and the adventure stories of Thomas Mayne Reid. Heavier reading included philosophic works that enjoyed a high reputation at the time, such as Buckle's positivist and sceptical survey of European culture, *The History of Civilisation in England.* Later in life, Chekhov took a wry view of this omnivorous autodidacticism, and had the clumsy bookkeeper Yepikhodov in *The Cherry Orchard* read Buckle for self-improvement.

It was at this time that Chekhov began writing, sending comic pieces to Aleksandr in Moscow in the hope they would be accepted by the numerous humour magazines that had sprung up in the capitals. He made friends with actors, hung around backstage, and learned how to make up. One of his school-fellows, Aleksandr Vishnevsky, did enter the profession, and eventually became a charter member of the Moscow Art Theatre. Nikolay Solovtsov, to whom Chekhov dedicated his farce *The Bear* and who created the title role, was another friend from these Taganrog days.

In 1879 Chekhov came to Moscow to study medicine at the University, aided by a scholarship from the Taganrog municipal authorities. He arrived to discover himself the head of the family, which was still in dire straits and living in a cramped basement flat in a disreputable slum. His father, now a humble clerk, boarded at his office; his elder brothers, Aleksandr, a writer, and Nikolay, a painter, led alcoholic bohemian lives; his three younger siblings, Ivan, Mariya, and Mikhail, had still to complete their educations. Lodging at home, Chekhov was compelled to launch a career as journalist, at the same time he carried out the rigorous five-year medical course.

At first, he wrote primarily for humour magazines, contributing anecdotes and extended jokes, sometimes as captions to Nikolay's drawings; these brought in ten to twelve kopeks a line. Gradually, he diversified into parodies, short stories and serials, including a murder mystery and a romance that proved so popular it was filmed four times in the early days of cinema. He was a reporter at a famous trial. He became close friends with Nikolay Leykin, editor of the periodical *Splinters* (*Oskolki*). He conducted a theatrical gossip column, which won him entry to all the greenrooms and side-scenes in Moscow. And he shared in his brothers' bohemianism; he wrote to an old schoolchum, in a letter the Soviets publish only in expurgated form: 'I was on the trot all last night and, 'cept for a 5-ruble drunk didn't . . . or catch . . . . I'm just about to go on the trot again'.[5] His writing at this time was published under a variety of pseudonyms, the best known Antosha Chekhonte, from a schoolboy nickname. He also found time to revise *Without Patrimony* which he seriously hoped would be staged; turned down by the leading actress to whom he submitted it, it was burnt by its author. But a copy survived, minus the title-page, and was first published in 1923; it has since become known as *Platonov*, after the central character.

1884 was a critical date in Chekhov's life. At the age of twenty-four, he set up as a general practitioner and, influenced by reading Herbert Spencer, began research on a history of medicine in Russia. Ironically, that December he had bouts of spitting blood, which his medical expertise might have diagnosed as symptoms of pulmonary tuberculosis. No outside observer would have suspected that this active, well-built, handsome man was suffering from a mortal illness. Only in his last years did he become a semi-invalid and, until that time, he maintained the pretence that his symptoms were not fatal. This subterfuge was not carried on simply to allay his family's fears. He wilfully strove to ignore the forecast of his own mortality.

1884 also saw his first published collection of stories, pointedly entitled *Fairy Tales of Melpomene*: the muse of tragedy compressed into pithy anecdotes of the life of actors. Chekhov had found more prestigious and better-paying periodicals to take his stories and was now an expert on Muscovite life.

He had an opportunity to amplify his subject matter, when he and his family began to spend summers in the country, first with his brother Ivan, master of a village school; then in a cottage on the estate of the Kiselev family. It was during these summers that Chekhov gained first-hand knowledge of the manor-house setting he employed in so many of his plays, and made the acquaintance of officers of a battery, who turn up in *Three Sisters*. Chekhov's artistic horizons also expanded, for the Kiselevs, intimates of Tchaikovsky, were devoted to classical music. Another summer visitor to become a lifelong friend was the painter Isaak Levitan, whose impressionistic landscapes are the painterly equivalent of Chekhov's prose techniques.

In 1885 Chekhov's literary career took a conscientious turn upwards. On a visit to St. Petersburg, he had been embarrassed by the acclaim that greeted him, because he recognised that he had been writing sloppily: 'If I had known that that was how they were reading me,' he told his brother Aleksandr (4 January 1886), 'I would not have written like a hack'. Shortly thereafter, he received a letter from D. V. Grigorovich, *doyen* of Russian critics, singling him out as the most promising writer of his time and urging him to take his talent more seriously. Although Antosha Chekhonte continued to appear in print for a few more years, Anton Chekhov made his first bow in the prestigious Petersburg newspaper *New Times* (*Novoe Vremya*). Its editor Aleksey Suvorin had risen from peasant origins to become a tycoon and leading influence-monger in the conservative political camp; he and Chekhov were to be closely allied, although their friendship would later founder when Suvorin promoted the anti-Semitic line during the Dreyfus affair.

During the years when he was winning recognition as a short-story writer, Chekov made two further attempts to write for the theatre. With the first, *On the High Way* (*Na bolshoy doroge*, 1885), he came up against the obstacle of the censorship, which banned it on the grounds that it was a 'gloomy, squalid play'. The other piece, the monologue *On the Harmfulness of Tobacco* (*O brede tabake*) was, like many of his early 'dramatic études', written with a specific actor in mind. It appeared in 1886 in a St. Petersburg newspaper, and Chekhov kept revising it, publishing the final version, almost a new work, in his collected writings of 1903. Two farces, *Hamlet Prince of Denmark* and *The Power of Hypnotism* (both 1887), never got beyond the planning stage.

Profiting from an advance from Suvorin, Chekhov returned to southern Russia in 1887, a refreshment of the memory that was productive of remarkable work. The stories that followed signalled his emergence as a leading writer of serious fiction. The publication of *The Steppe*

(*Step*, 1888) took place in *The Northern Herald* (*Severny vestnik*), one of those so-called 'fat' journals that had housed the works of Turgenev and Tolstoy, and were instruments of public opinion. That same year, Chekhov was awarded the Pushkin Prize for Literature by the Imperial Academy of Science for his collection *In the Gloaming* (*V sumerkakh*). One of the most enthusiastic instigators of this honour had been the writer Vladimir Nemirovich-Danchenko, who would later play an important role in establishing Chekhov's reputation as a dramatist.

The Northern Herald was liberal in its politics, its editor Aleksey Pleshcheyev having been a prisoner in Siberia with Dostoevsky. Typically, Chekhov was able to be friends with Pleshcheyev and Suvorin simultaneously, and he continued to write for *New Times*. But this reluctance to identify himself with a party exposed him to much acrimonious criticism from members of both camps, and especially from the progressive left. Katherine Mansfield has pointed out that the 'problem' in literature is an invention of the nineteenth century; one of the legacies of Russian 'civic criticism' of the 1840s was the notion that a writer had both an obligation to depict social problems and to pose a solution, making his works an uplifting tool of enlightenment. This usually meant espousing a doctrinaire political platform. Chekhov, perhaps fortified by his medical training, treasured his objectivity and steadfastly refrained from taking sides, even when his sympathies were easy to ascertain. 'God keep us from generalisations,' he wrote. 'There are a great many opinions in this world and a good half of them are professed by people who have never had any problems'.

Between 1886 and 1890, his letters chew the cud over objectivity and his 'monthly change' of opinions, which readers preferred to see as the views of his leading characters. To his brother Aleksandr (10 May 1886), he insisted that no undue emphasis be placed on political, social or economic questions in writing. The author must be an observer, posing questions, but not supplying the answers, he insisted to Suvorin (27 October 1888); it is the reader who brings subjectivity to bear. Not that an author should be cold, but his own involvement in a problem should be unglimpsed by the reader.

> You reproach me for my objectivity, [he wrote to Suvorin, 1 April 1890] calling it indifference to good and evil, absence of ideals and ideas, etc. You want me to say, when I depict horsethieves: horse-stealing is a bad thing. But that's been known for a long time, without my help, hasn't it? Let juries pass verdicts on horse-thieves; as for me, my work is only to show them as they are.

The year before *The Steppe* appeared, Chekhov had at last had a play produced; the impresario Fyodor Korsh had commissioned *Ivanov* and staged it at his Moscow theatre on 19 November 1887. It was an outstanding if controversial success. 'Theatre-buffs say they've never seen so much ferment, so much unanimous applause-*cum*-hissing, and never ever heard so many arguments as they saw and heard at my play' (To Aleksandr, 20 November 1887). It was taken up by the Alexandra Theatre, the Imperial playhouse in St. Petersburg, and produced there on 31 January 1889, after much hectic rewriting in an attempt to make the playwright's intentions clearer and to take into account the strengths and weaknesses of the new cast.

Secure in his reputation and income at the age of thirty, Chekhov made the surprising move of travelling ten thousand miles to Sakhalin, the Russian Devil's Island, in

1890; the journey alone was arduous, for the Trans-Siberian Railway had not yet been built. The enterprise may have been inspired by a Tolstoy-influenced desire to practice a new-found altruism. In any case, the ensuing documentary study of the penal colony was a model of impartial field research and may have led to prison reforms. On a more personal level, it intensified a new strain of pessimism in Chekhov's work, for, despite his disclaimers, he began to be bothered by his lack of outlook or mission. The death of his brother Nikolay and his own failing health led him to question the dearth of ideals or motives in his writing. *A Boring Story* (*Skuchnaya istoriya*, 1889) initiated this phase, with its first-person narrative of frustrated ideals and isolation.

The steady flow of royalties enabled Chekhov in 1891 to buy a farmstead at Melikhovo, some fifty miles south of Moscow, where he settled his parents and siblings. There he set about 'to squeeze the last drop of slave out of his system' (to Suvorin, 7 January 1899); 'a modern Cincinnatus,' he planted a cherry orchard and became a lavish host. This rustication had a beneficial effect on both his literary work and his humanitarianism. He threw himself into schemes for road-building, ameliorating peasant life, establishing schools and other improvements; during the cholera epidemic of 1892–93, he acted as an overworked member of the sanitary commission and head of the famine relief board. These experiences found their way into the character of Dr. Astrov in *Uncle Vanya*.

During this period, Chekhov composed masterful novellas that explored the dead ends of life: *The Duel* (*Duel*), *Ward No. 6* (*Palata No. 6*), *The Black Monk* (*Chyorny monakh*), *The Teacher of Literature* (*Uchitel slovesnosti*), *The House with the Maisonette* (*Dom s mezaninom*), *My Life* (*Moya zhizn*) and *Peasants* (*Muzhiki*), carefully wrought prose pieces of great psychological subtlety. They recurrently dwell on the illusions indispensable to making life bearable, the often frustrated attempts at contact with one's fellow-man, the inexorable pull of inertia preventing humans from realising their potential for honesty and happiness. Chekhov's attitude is clinically critical, but always with a keen eye for the sympathetic detail that leads the reader to deeper awareness.

The success of *Ivanov* and the curtain-raisers, *The Bear* (*Medved*) and *The Proposal* (*Predlozhenie*) (1888–89), had put Chekhov at a premium as a dramatist. Urged on by Korsh and others, and frustrated by abortive projects for a novel, Chekhov plugged away at the comedy *The Wood Demon* (*Leshy*). It was promptly turned down by the state-subsidised theatres of Petersburg and Moscow which regarded it as more a dramatised story than a genuine play; they recommended that Chekhov give up writing for the theatre. A production at Abramova's Theatre in Moscow was received with apathy bordering on contempt, and may have confirmed Chekhov's decision to go to Sakhalin. For some years he did abandon the theatre, except for a one-act farce *The Jubilee* (*Yubiley*, 1891) and an unfinished comedy, *The Night Before the Trial* (*Noch pered suda*).

Not until January 1894 did he announce that he had again begun a play, only to renounce it a year later: 'I am not writing a play and I don't feel like writing one. I've grown old and I've lost my spark. I'd rather like to write a novel a hundred miles long' (to V. V. Bilibin, 18 January 1895). A year and a half later he was to break the news, '. . . can you imagine, I'm writing a play. . . it gives me a certain pleasure, although I rebel dreadfully against the conventions of the stage. It's a comedy, three female roles, six male roles, a landscape (view of a lake); lots of talk about literature, little action, a ton of love' (to Suvorin, 21 October 1895).

This comedy was *The Seagull* (*Chayka*), which had a rocky opening night at the Alexandra Theatre in 1896: the actors misunderstood it, the audience misapprehended it. Despite protestations of unconcern – 'I dosed myself with castor oil, took a cold bath – and now I wouldn't even mind writing another play' (to Suvorin, 22 October 1896) – Chekhov fled to Moscow, where he cultivated a distaste for writing for the stage. Although *The Seagull* grew in public favour in subsequent performances, Chekhov disliked submitting his work to the judgment of literary cliques and claques. Yet barely one year after this event, a new drama appeared in the 1897 collection of his plays: *Uncle Vanya* (*Dyadya Vanya*), a reworking of *The Wood Demon*; and he began to draft the play that became *Three Sisters* (*Tri sestry*).

Chekhov's illness was definitively diagnosed as tuberculosis in 1897, and he was compelled to leave Melikhovo for a milder climate. For the rest of his life, he shuttled between Yalta on the Black Sea and various French and German spas. To pay these new expenses, Chekhov sold all he had written before 1899, excepting the plays, to the publisher Marks for 75,000 rubles, along with the reprint rights to any future stories. It was an improvident move, since Marks had had no idea of the number of Chekhov's works. This error in calculation may have induced Chekhov to concentrate on playwriting which would prove to be more profitable.

The remainder of his dramatic career was bound up with the fortunes of the Moscow Art Theatre, founded in 1897 by his friend Nemirovich-Danchenko and the wealthy dilettante K. S. Alekseyev who acted under the name Stanislavsky. Chekhov was one of the original shareholders in the enterprise, for he admired their announced programme of ensemble playing, a serious attitude to art, and plays of high literary quality; at the opening production, Aleksey Tolstoy's blank-verse historical drama *Tsar Fyodor Ioannovich*, his eye was caught by Olga Knipper, the young actress who played the Tsarina. With only slight misgiving Chekhov allowed the Art Theatre to revive *The Seagull* at the close of its first season; Stanislavsky, the co-director, had greater misgivings, for he did not understand the play. But a strong cast and a heavily atmospheric production won over the audience, and the play had a resounding success. The Moscow Art Theatre adopted an art-nouveau seagull as its insignia and henceforth regarded itself as the House of Chekhov. When the Maly Theatre insisted on revisions to *Uncle Vanya* Chekhov withdrew the play and allowed the Art Theatre to stage its premiere, along with a revival of *Ivanov*. *Three Sisters* (1901) was written with Moscow Art actors in mind.

Chekhov's chronic reaction to the production of his plays was revulsion, and so two months after the opening of *Three Sisters*, he was writing 'I myself am quite discarding the theatre, I'll never write another thing for it. One can write for the theatre in Germany, Sweden, even Spain, but not in Russia, where dramatic authors aren't respected, are kicked with hooves and never forgiven success or failure' (to Olga Knipper, 1 March 1901). Nevertheless, he soon was deep into *The Cherry Orchard* (*Vyshnyovy sad*, 1904), tailoring the roles to specific Moscow Art players. Each of these productions won Chekhov greater fame as a playwright, even when he himself disagreed with the chosen interpretation of the Moscow Art Theatre. Not long before his death, he was contemplating yet another play, this one even more untraditional, in which an Arctic explorer would be visited by the ghost of his beloved, and a ship would be seen crushed by ice.

At the age of forty, Chekhov married Olga Knipper. His liaisons with women had been numerous but low-keyed. He exercised an involuntary fascination over a certain type of ambitious bluestocking, who saw him as her mentor and herself as his Egeria. But whenever the affair became too demanding or the woman too clinging, Chekhov would use irony and playful humour to disengage himself. In his writings, marriage is usually portrayed as a snare and a delusion that mires his characters in spirit-sapping vulgarity. His relationship with Olga Knipper was both high-spirited – she was his 'kitten,' his 'puppy,' his 'lambkin,' his 'darling crocodile' – and conveniently aloof, for she had to spend much of her time in Moscow, while he convalesced at his villa in Yalta. On these terms, the marriage was a success.

The home in Yalta (today a Soviet museum) became a Mecca for young writers, importunate fans, touring acting companies, and plain free-loaders. Such pilgrimages, though well meant, did not conduce to Chekhov's peace of mind or body, and his health continued to deteriorate. In December 1903, he came to Moscow to attend rehearsals of *The Cherry Orchard*; the opening night, 17 January 1904, coincided with his nameday and the twenty-fifth anniversary of the commencement of his literary activity. Emaciated, hunched over, gravely ill, he did not show up until the second act and was made to stay through Act Three when the ceremony to honour him took place, greatly to his surprise.

Despite his rapid decline in health and the disappointment of Olga's miscarriage in 1902, a deeply lyrical tone enters his last writings. His final stories, *Lady with Lapdog* (*Dama s sobachkoy*), *The Archbishop* (*Arkhierey*), and *The Darling* (*Dushenka*) present a more accepting view of the cyclical nature of life. They also reveal an almost musical

14

attention to the structure and sounds of words, to be remarked as well in that last 'comedy' *The Cherry Orchard*.

In June 1904 his doctors ordered Chekhov to Baden-weiler, a small health resort in the Black Forest. There the forty-four-year old writer died on July 2. Shortly before his death, the doctor recommended putting an ice pack on his heart. 'You don't put ice on an empty heart,' Chekhov protested. When they insisted that he drink champagne, his last words came, 'It's been a long time sinced I've drunk champagne'. He was unconsciously echoing the line of the old nurse Marina in *Uncle Vanya*, 'It's a long time since I've tasted noodles'. Chekhov's obsequies were a comedy of errors he might have appreciated: the railway carriage that bore his body to St Petersburg was stencilled with the label 'Fresh Oysters,' and at the Moscow cemetery, the bystanders spent more time ogling Maksim Gorky and the basso Chaliapin than in mourning.[6] Inadvertently, the procession became entangled with that of General Keller, a military hero who had been shipped home from the Far East, and Chekhov's friends were startled to hear an army band accompanying the remains of a man who had always been chary of grand gestures.

2
At the Play

'It is easy to convince the sentimental and credulous populace that the theatre, such as it is, is a school. But anyone who knows what a school is will not fall for this bait. I don't know what will happen fifty or a hundred years from now, but in its present state the theatre can only serve as an amusement.' *The first-person narrator of* **A Boring Story**, *1889*

After his family moved to Moscow, Chekhov the schoolboy became an inveterate spectator at the Taganrog Civic Theatre, in company with his enthusiastic uncle Mitrofan. At this very time, the Taganrog management had completely refurbished the repertory to suit a new building constructed in 1865. Formerly, the local company had played an outworn stock of Kotzebue and Pixérécourt, Lensky's vaudevilles and the grandiloquent patriotic dramas of Polevoy. The new management endeavoured to introduce the Taganrog public to more ambitious fare, enabling them to see Italian opera, along with Gogol's *Inspector General* and *Getting Married*, and the 'new

16

drama' of Ostrovsky, Potekhin, Dyachenko, and Shpazhinsky. The newness now seems tenuous as Dyachenko's society dramas are one step away from *Lady Audley's Secret*, but as an impressionable adolescent, Chekhov observed what was taken to be the latest thing – problem plays, peasant dramas, and comedies of *byt* or everyday life, full of brutish merchants, virtuous muzhiks and improvident nobles. He also cherished a fondness for the older varieties of romantic melodrama, such as Dumas' *Kean*, and *The Mail Robbery* (the Russian *Lyons Mail*), which turns up in *The Seagull* as a memory of Shamraev the anecdotal overseer.

In 1873, when Chekhov was thirteen, the Taganrog management featured comic operas by Lecocq and Offenbach: the latter's *La Belle Hélène*, the first play Chekhov ever saw, was probably the most popular stage work in Tsarist Russia, and crops up repeatedly in Chekhov's writing. If we examine the repertory lists for 1876–79, when we know that Chekhov resorted regularly to the theatre to solace his loneliness, we find that he could have seen, among other presentations, four plays of Ostrovsky, a play apiece by Sardou and Dennery, one by Dyachenko, Offenbach's *Périchole* and Dargomyzhsky's *Rusalka*, a reference to which also surfaces in *The Seagull*.[1] The actors who played in these pieces belonged to a generation of flamboyant personalities who held an audience rapt by the virtuosity of their playing, little subordinated to the script.

For all its deficiencies, Chekhov could comprehend the appeal of the 'new drama', though he never put much stock in its attempts at social relevance and verisimilitude. At the same time, he mocked the conservatives who decried stage realism and hearkened back to the romantic past. In *On Drama* (1884), he showed a callous provincial magistrate pontificating on art:

Present-day dramatists and actors strive, uh, how can I put this more clearly . . . they strive to be life-like, realistic . . . On stage you see what you see in life . . . But is that what we need? We need expression, impact! [. . .] An actor used to talk with an unnatural gruff voice, beat his breast with his fists, howl, drop to the ground, and yet how expressive he was! And he was expressive in his speeches too! He would talk about duty, humanity, freedom. . .[2]

The impresario in the story *The Jubilee* (1886) declares that art is dead, because 'Today it's the thing to say the stage needs truth to life! . . . You can see that anywhere: at the inn, at home, in the market, but at the theatre give me expressiveness!'[3] In fact, the new problem plays did retain enough of the romantic melodrama's emotionalism and rant to satisfy ordinary audiences.

Chekhov's years as a medical student in Moscow coincided with a period of transition in the drama. Increasing pressure from Ostrovsky and amateur groups for 'people's' theatres had led to the cancellation in 1882 of the monopoly held by the Imperial theatres. Many private theatricals went professional, appealing to new audiences and creating showcases for new playwrights, homegrown and imported. The young theatres Chekhov regularly attended were those of the 'Muscovite wizards and warlocks', Mikhail Lentovsky and Fyodor Korsh, who, in their separate ways, promulgated 'new forms'.

Chekhov's brother Nikolay worked for Lentovsky as a scene-painter, so they had free entry to the Hermitage Pleasure Garden, which he managed, and its 'Fantasy Theatre', a derelict mansion overgrown with weeds, but rendered romantic by moonbeams and electric fairy lights, chimes, a hidden orchestra, and a small stage where

Lentovsky could present the latest music hall attractions from Paris and Vienna. In 1886, with money from the merchant class that supported him, Lentovsky founded the Skomorokh or Mountebank Theatre, hoping to present a prestigious repertory. He even negotiated with Tolstoy, a supporter of 'people's' theatre, to mount *The Power of Darkness*, but the censor forbade it. Plays of Gogol and Ostrovsky and even *Hamlet* could be found there, but gradually the bulk of the repertory was translated farces, melodramas and *féeries*, including the Offenbach–Verne *Trip to the Moon* with illuminated panoramas. Lentovsky's productions abounded in pyrotechnical displays, explosions, fires, collapsing bridges, and the whole impedimenta of sensationalism. Of *The Forest Tramp* (1883), Chekhov wrote, 'Thanks to this new, bitter-sweet, German Liebergottic rubbish all Moscow smells of gunpowder'.[4]

Although his personal relations with Lentovsky, whom he credited with some sense and ingenuity, were good, Chekhov filled his newspaper columns with hilarious sallies at the mixtures of fustian and flash powder the director served up. He composed two absurd skits, *Unclean Tragedians and Leprous Playwrights* and *A Mess in Rome* (both 1884), which riotously flayed the entrepreneur's choice of material, stagecraft and actors. Basically Chekhov's complaint was that Lentovsky's extravaganzas compromised heightened realism with flashy trickery; they were junkfood rather than true nourishment for the imagination. When Lentovskyan fireworks explode in a play of Chekhov's like *Planonov*, they are there to contrast with the damp squibs of the characters' unachieved yearnings.

At his theatre, which opened in 1882 with *The Inspector General*, the former lawyer and ticket broker Korsh maintained a stable of hacks to produce translations of European bedroom farce and well-carpentered dramas of adultery; by so doing, he greatly increased his audiences and reached ranks of society new to the theatre. Moreover, to his credit, he instituted a policy of matinees at reduced prices every Friday, when he would present classics and controversial new plays. A Korsh première normally drew the entire literary and artistic world of Moscow, as well as an enthusiastic younger generation. Stanislavsky attributed to him the creation, over a decade, of a theatrically sophisticated public that was ready to accept the reforms of the Moscow Art Theatre.

Important works such as *The Power of Darkness*, Ibsen's *A Doll's House* and *An Enemy of the People*, and plays by Becque, Rostand and Sudermann had their first Moscow productions at Korsh matinees, in elaborate stage settings renowned for their realism. It was Korsh who nagged at Chekhov to write a comedy in the spirit of his funny stories, and who produced Chekhov's first staged play, *Ivanov*, with great success. Korsh's theatre, with its dedicated if uneven acting company, naturalistic scenery and lip service to the higher ideals of drama may be the generic target of Treplyov's disgust in *The Seagull* at the 'cliché-ridden, pedestrian' modern theatre.

> When the curtain goes up to reveal an artificially-lighted room with three walls, these great talents, high priests of sacred art, demonstrate how people eat, drink, love, walk, wear their jackets; when out of cheap, vulgar tableaux and cheap, vulgar speeches they try to extract a moral – a tiny little moral, easy to understand, useful around the house; when in a thousand different ways they serve up the same old thing over and over again – then I run and keep on running . . . (Act 1)

During the period when Korsh and Lentovsky dominated the Moscow scene, Chekhov's journalism entailed much theatre attendance, and he became acquainted with actors and managers. Familiarity bred contempt in him but could not efface his perennial fascination with the stage. Many of his early works teem with vignettes of backstage life, usually presented as caricatures or sardonic social commentary. There is nothing idealised about Chekhov's gallery of thespians, who are depicted as vain, ignorant, petty but somehow more sympathetic than the solid citizenry. In the late 1880s, when Chekhov's friendship with professional playwrights such as Shcheglov (Leontyev) and Prince Sumbatov (Yuzhin) deepened, and when he saw his own plays produced, his commentary grew more embittered, more caustic and more exasperated. 'Actors are capricious and conceited,' he wrote to Leykin (4 December 1887), 'half-educated and presumptuous,' and, to Suvorin, 'actresses are cows who fancy themselves goddesses' (17 December 1889).

> Actors never observe ordinary people. They do not know landowners or merchants or village priests or bureaucrats. On the other hand they can give distinguished impersonations of billiard markers, kept women, distressed cardsharps, in short all those individuals whom they observe as they ramble through pothouses and bachelor parties. Horrible ignorance (to Suvorin, 25 November 1889).

When Suvorin proposed to buy a theatre in St. Petersburg, Chekhov tried vainly to dissuade him. But once Suvorin's Theatre was a *fait accompli*, Chekhov showered his friend with advice, recommendations, and suggestions for casting. In particular, he boosted Lidiya Yavorskaya, a popular star who excelled in plays such as *La Dame aux caméllias* and *Madame Sans-Gêne.* Chekhov's brother Mikhail later wrote, 'I was never a fan of her talent and especially disliked her voice, screechy and cracked as if she had a chronic sore throat. But she was an intelligent woman, progressive, and for her benefits would stage plays that seemed at the time "racy".'[5] Chekhov was well aware of her defects as an actress, but they had a very brief fling, and he later used some of her traits in sketching Arkadina in *The Seagull.*

As his intimacy with professionals grew, Chekhov commented even more impatiently about the theatre's shortcomings. 'I implore you,' he wrote to Shcheglov, 'please fall out of love with the stage'.

> True, there is a lot of good in it. The good is overstated to the skies, and the vileness is masked . . . The modern theatre is a rash, an urban disease. The disease must be swept away, and loving it is unhealthy. You start arguing with me, repeating the old phrase, the theatre is a school, it educates and so on . . . But I am telling you what I see: the modern theatre is not superior to the crowd; on the contrary, the life of the crowd is more elevated and intelligent than the theatre . . . (25 November 1888, 20 December 1888)

A typical example of what Chekhov abhorred in the theatre of his time was *The Fumes of Life*, Boleslav Markevich's dramatisation of his fashionable novel *The Abyss* (1883). It became such a *bête noir* that he returned to attack it again and again, excoriating it as a 'long, fat boring ink-blot' 'as pleasant as yesterday's porridge';[6] he wrote a parody of *The Fumes of Life*, but had it destroyed in proof. His review of Lentovsky's production was unacharacteristically abusive and personal, and ended, 'On the whole, the play is written with a lavatory brush and smells foul'.

The play that provoked such an intense reaction is a tear-jerker in the style of Dumas *fils*. It features an adventuress, who, over the course of five acts, betrays her adoring husband with his best friend, is protected and then repudiated by a noble old Count, becomes a pariah in Petersburg society, weds a scoundrel who robs and abandons her, and at last dies in an odour of sanctity, repentant and contrite, declaring that her life has been nothing but delusive 'fumes'. A role that involves five costume changes, the opportunity to run the gamut from passion to piety, and an almost constant presence on stage would have immediate appeal to the Yavorskayas. In *The Seagull*, Chekhov has Arkadina tour this play in the provinces well into the mid-nineties, thus making a sarcastic reflection on her taste and vanity.

Partly it is a question of technique: twenty years later Ranevskaya in *The Cherry Orchard* is as 'depraved' as the heroine of *The Fumes of Life*, with her callous lover and her chequered past. But Chekhov keeps the sensational events offstage, while he shows us other, more everyday facets of her character. The most popular dramatist of Chekhov's day was the prolific hack Viktor Krylov, notorious for crass sentimentality. When Chekhov's *Ivanov* was in rehearsal in 1887, Krylov offered to doctor the play to meet acceptable stage standards, in return for a fifty per cent cut of the profits. Chekhov politely refused, not least because the entire goal of his dramatic activity was to deny the validity of those standards.[7]

Recoiling from the banality of the contemporary stage and its over-indulgence in cheap morality and flashy effects, Chekhov was among the first Russian writers to be attracted to symbolist drama. In the early 1890s, Dmitry

23

Merezhkovsky called for a return to liturgy in the drama, to produce a quasi-religious elation in the spectator; symbols rather than images were to be the effective artistic tool. Vladimir Solovyov's popular doctrine of a 'world soul' was translated into theatrical terms as a communion of audience with player; the playwright's creative will was to lift the spectator beyond the material world into a transcendental realm. For models, the symbolists turned to Henrik Ibsen, whose characters they interpreted as abstractions conducive to radiant visions, and to Maurice Maeterlinck, who insisted that a play's action be internalised and submerged. In this aesthetic, individual character became less important than the struggle with a higher destiny. 'The essence of drama,' Merezhkovsky proclaimed in 1894, 'is the battle of a conscious will with obstacles'. The earliest Russian symbolist drama is Nikolay Minsky's mystery play, *Cold Words* (1896), which is in modern dress but otherwise every bit as recondite and 'undramatic' as Treplyov's play in *The Seagull*, written the same year.

Chekhov disparaged the symbolists' metaphysical pretensions, and they later returned the favour by reviling his plays for their depressing 'cold wind from the abyss.'[9] But Chekhov was not disdainful of their literary experimentation. Although, as both Stanislavsky and Olga Knipper attest, he regarded Ibsen as neither lifelike nor stage worthy, 'complicated, involved and cerebral,'[10] Chekhov was attracted to Maeterlinck's 'odd wonderful plays [which] make an enormous impression'. What impressed him seems to have been their theatrical flair; mystical doctrines mattered less than that a play should work on stage. A week before he completed *The Seagull*, he had suggested that Suvorin stage Maeterlinck at his Petersburg theatre. 'If I were your producer, in two years I would turn it into a decadent playhouse or try my hand at doing so. The theatre might perhaps look strange, but still it would have a personality' (2 November 1895). (But he was not doctrinaire; in the same letter, he also recommended Zola's *Thérèse Raquin*.) What he especially liked in *Les Aveugles* was 'a splendid set with the sea and a lighthouse in the distance' (to Suvorin, 12 July 1897). Maêterlinck appealed to Chekhov not for his other worldly creed, but for his stagecraft, his 'new forms'.

In letters to would-be dramatists, Chekhov continually came back to the need to see and understand how plays worked in the theatre. He was reluctantly compelled to reject Bjørnstjerne Bjørnson's spiritual drama *Beyond Human Power*, which he found moving and intelligent, because 'it won't do for the stage, because it can't be played, there's no action, no living characters, no dramatic interest' (To Suvorin, 20 June 1896). (Incidentally, this is the same argument Nina advances against Treplyov's play in *The Seagull*.) However, no cohesive theory of drama is to be cobbled together from Chekhov's voluminous correspondence. When scrutinised closely, his criticism turns out to be hints on craft: 'avoid clichés,' 'be compact,' 'use realistic dialogue,' 'vary the characters,' 'put your climax in the third act but be sure the fourth is not anticlimactic. . .'. His eminently practical comments on Gorky's plays, for example, have to do with their effects on an audience and how 'points' are to be made. Even his references to his own plays are meant to clarify particulars for the performers or react to specific performances. His legendary statement that 'on stage people dine, simply dine, and meanwhile their happiness is taking shape or their lives are breaking up'[11] is indeed a telegraphic synopsis of an aesthetic, but it is a symbolist aesthetic: beyond the commonplace surface of existing lurks the real life of the characters.

When Chekhov himself set about to write plays, he was

torn between creating works that would be successful because of their conformity to accepted norms, and works that avoided the clichés and conventions of the popular stage. He also had to confront the fact that audiences expected the dramatic equivalents of his prose writings, either hilarious anecdotes or refined treatments of modern life. When *The Seagull* failed in St. Petersburg in 1896, one spectator observed that the reasons for its failure were manifold.[12] It exasperated the older generation of literary men by its novelty. It exasperated the younger writers by what seemed to them Chekhov's failure to write a purely symbolic drama. It annoyed the journalists who associated Chekhov with Suvorin and *New Times* and would attack any members of that faction.

The development of Chekhov's drama then progresses from a gradual liberation from the theatre's traditional demands to the expression of an idiosyncratic and original vision. Chekhov had to find a way to convey the subtlety and multi-layered nature of his compressed fiction into drama, which has no narrative. It is no coincidence, perhaps, that Chekhov's earlier efforts, those most wedded to the conventions of the problem play and current stage practice, were composed while he was deeply immersed in the literary life of the Russian capitals. As early as 1887, Chekhov was insisting that the author must control his play, select the cast and issue instructions for its production (to N. A. Leykin, 15 November 1887).

The first consistent example of his new art, *Uncle Vanya*, was the deliberate revision of a failed experiment; his first perfectly-orchestrated achievement, *Three Sisters*, was written for the Moscow Art Theatre, a company made up of educated individuals, devoted to ensemble playing and the evocation of 'mood'. *The Cherry Orchard*, a work whose shape breaks with both realistic social drama and the Art

Theatre's soulful atmospherics, would be written in Yalta
far distant from the day-to-day activities of a theatre and
the call of literary fashion.

3
Journeyman Efforts

I don't believe in our intelligentsia . . . I believe in individual
people, I see salvation in individual personalities . . . *Chekhov, to
Ivan Orlov (22 February 1889)*

The hammy hand of the contemporary Russian stage lay
most heavily on Chekhov's earliest dramatic endeavours.
The three full-length plays that preceded *The Seagull*
reveal how Chekhov gradually mastered the dramatic form
and how he sought to remodel it according to his own
needs.

'Without Patrimony' ('Platonov')

While still in high school, Chekhov wrote a four-act play so
full of incident, 'with horse-stealing a gunshot, a woman
who throws herself under a train',[1] that a family friend
described it as a 'drrama', the two 'r's' bespeaking its
sensationalism. The critical consensus today regards it as
the first draft of the work now known as *Platonov*.

Hopefully, the neophyte author sent the play, entitled *Without Patrimony*, to his literary brother Aleksandr in Moscow, and got back this critique (14 October 1878):

> In without patrimony two scenes are worked out ingeniously, if you like, but on the whole it is an inexcusable, albeit innocent lie. Innocent because it derives from the virginal depths of your inner view of the world. You must feel yourself, though faintly and involuntarily, that your drama is a lie ... The handling and the dramatic talent are worthy (on your own part) of greater activity and a wider frame.[2]

Chekhov must have taken this to heart, for he continued to work on the play; toning down the dialogue, dropping two characters (Shcherbuk's ugly daughters), and omitting a lurid scene in which Voynitsev pulled a dagger on Platonov, who disarmed him with the shout 'Stand back!' and a torrent of rhetoric. Even with cuts, it was twice the length of the average play of the period. But Chekhov took it to Mariya Yermolova, one of the stars of the Moscow Maly Theatre, as a possible offering for an upcoming benefit performance. The addressee was ill-considered: the only part suitable for Yermolova's status would have been that of Anna Petrovna, the frivolous widow, besieged on all sides by admirers. Yermolova was noted for her heroic impersonations of Joan of Arc and Lady Macbeth; her roles seldom admitted sexual laxity. In any case, she returned the play, and the chagrined young playwright tore up the manuscript.

But his brother Mikhail had copied out two scripts for submission to the censorship; and one of these survived to be published in 1923. Since then, actors and producers have tried to reconstitute it for the stage as a 'newly discovered play by Chekhov'. Cut to the bone, it has, since the 1930s, appeared as *A Country Scandal*, *A Provincial Don Juan*, and, most frequently, as *Platonov*. Probably the most distinguished attempts were those of Jean Vilar in 1956, under the title *Ce Fou Platonov*, and Michael Frayn's wholly rewritten 1984 version *Wild Honey*. None of these versions has managed to secure a place for the protracted piece of juvenilia in the repertory. Its interest resides primarily in its being a dramatic storehouse for Chekhov's later themes and characters. Most intricately re-worked of all, the threat that the estate is to be auctioned in *Platonov* was to become the connecting thread and constitutive symbol of *The Cherry Orchard*.

A sign of Chekhov's youth at the time of writing is the obsession with parental relations, emblazoned in the original title *Without Patrimony* (*Bezottsovshchina*). Specifically, it refers to the economic dispossession of the main characters: Platonov, a member of the gentry, is forced by circumstances to descend in caste by becoming a village schoolmaster; Voynitsev loses the family estate through his stepmother's extravagance. But a bleak picture is drawn of fathers and children on a moral level as well. Platonov's recollections of his late father are contemptuous and angry. Glagolyev Junior heartlessly tricks his father and provokes him to a stroke; both Glagolyevs woo the same woman unsuccessfully and drown their defeat in mutual debauchery in Paris. The Triletskys are ashamed of their old father, the General, whom they treat as a kind of wayward child. Shcherbuk hates his two daughters. Platonov's infant son is a source of ill-concealed annoyance. Only the Vengerovichs father and son seem to preserve a mutually respectful alliance, and they are Jews, outsiders in this society.

Chekhov was unable to pursue all the hares he started in

this play, or to find the proper angle of vision by which to regard his protagonist. Awkwardly, he puts his own opinion in the mouth of Glagolyev Senior shortly before Platonov makes his first entrance.

> Platonov, to my mind, is the best representative of modern uncertainty . . . He is the hero of the best, still, regrettably, unwritten modern novel . . . (*Laughs.*) By uncertainty I mean the current state of our society: the Russian man of letters can sense this uncertainty. He's come to an impasse, he's gone astray, he doesn't know what to focus on, doesn't understand . . . It's hard to understand these gentlemen, indeed it is!

The uncertainty is Chekhov's as well.

The rural Don Juan irresistible to women is also a cracker-barrel Schopenhauer whose alleged idealism and scepticism appeal to the men. Shallow and wishy-washy, he has a silver tongue, not unlike Turgenev's Rudin, the classic example of the *lishny chelovek* or superfluous man in Russian literature. He bears all the earmarks of the type: alienated, hypersensitive and mired in inertia, in direct succession to Lermontov's Pechorin, the Byronic 'hero of our times', and Griboyedov's drawing-room misanthrope Chatsky, who were characterized at least by a definite moral stance towards their imperfect society.

The squalour of his provincial community is hardly enough to justify Platonov's sense of superiority; he appears to have no ideals outside his own creature comforts. Did Chekhov intend a send-up of the superfluous man? Characteristically, he would make his initial forays into a new genre by parodying it. His first experiments with a 'long short story' were *The Futile Victory* (1882), a spoof of the popular Hungarian romancer Mór Jókai, and *A*

Hunting Drama (1884), a detective story in the style of Gaboriau. If *Platonov* is meant as parody, that would save it from being a failed attempt at a society melodrama in the style of Shpazhinsky or Dyachenko. Then again, it may not be a case of either/or: the immature dramatist was unsure of the direction to take. He may have seriously intended to explore certain social issues, but was ineluctably drawn to the comic side of things. He himself was aware of the ambivalence: 'However much I try to be serious, I don't succeed, in me the serious is constantly mixed up with the vulgar. I suppose it's my fatality' (to Yakov Polonsky, 22 February 1888).

Even if Platonov were a serious try at a 'superfluous man,' the type could not hold up when juxtaposed with closely-observed real life. Irony swamps Platonov's claims to heroic stature; under the microscope, he looks shoddy and despicable. Platonov himself is prone to making high-flown comparisons, fancying himself Hamlet, 'a second Byron' and 'a prospective Cabinet minister and a Christopher Columbus'; but he is somewhat shamefaced to reveal his paunchy schoolmaster presence to a former girlfriend who had put him on a pedestal. He has not even graduated from the university, although this does not prevent him from lecturing others on their spiritual and moral failings. Since most of the men in the community are grotesque buffoons or flaccid weaklings, he seems in contrast a paragon, and hence a lodestone to women.

Four of the *mille e tre* this village Don Giovanni numbers in his catalogue of conquests are drawn in detail. His wife Sasha is a long-suffering homebody, whom he forces to read Sacher-Masoch's *Ideals of Our Times.*[3] Sasha waits long hours for Platonov to return from parties, and when her nose is rubbed in his unfaithfulness, she twice attempts suicide. Chekhov is unable to withhold a smile from repeated suicide attempts, so that Sasha's laying herself on the railway tracks and then drinking an infusion of sulphur matches are more farcical than pathetic. Twenty-year-old Mariya Grekova is first offended by Platonov's brutal behaviour, then secretly smitten; and when he writes her an irresistibly abject letter of apology, she melts at once and abandons her lawsuit against him. The sophisticated widow Anna Petrovna openly puts herself on offer, and when she finds that he has made her daughter-in-law Sofiya his mistress, deals with the facts coolly, refusing to break off their liaison. Sofiya, the most deeply committed, having jeopardized her marriage and compelled Platonov to elope with her, finally, in a fit of jealousy on seeing him and Mariya together, takes up a handy pistol and shoots the philanderer. If Mariya is the Donna Elvira, then Sofiya is the Donna Anna of this prose opera.

Osip the horse-thief does not play Leporello to Platonov's Giovanni; rather, he is a kind of double on the plebeian plane. Chekhov is not very indulgent to the lower classes in this play; Anna's servants are lazy and insolent, preliminary sketches for Yasha in *The Cherry Orchard*. Marko the messenger from the district court is dense, if honest. But Osip, like Platonov, tries to set himself above his fellows, keenly appreciative of his own intelligence. 'Let's say ever'body knows, let's say, that I'm a thief and a robber too,' Osip laughs, 'but not ever'body can prove it . . . Hm . . . These plain folks don't dare nowadays, they're fools, no brains I mean . . . Scared of ever'thing . . .' 'A nasty underhanded, puny bunch . . . Ignoramuses . . . Don't feel sorry if folks like that git hurt.' Osip prides himself, as does Platonov, on being superior to his fellows, but his superiority is expressed in a sub-Nietzschean amorality. He hires himself out as an assassin and sets on nocturnal pedestrians, the criminal equivalent of

Platonov's egoistic manipulation of others' feelings. At the end, both are destroyed by the people they contemned: Osip is lynched by the peasants, and Platonov is shot by a cast-off mistress. The similarities are so great that when Platonov and Osip grapple in the schoolroom, it is like a man fighting his shadow or mystic double. Perhaps Osip reneges on the murder contract because he recognizes their symbiosis.

For all its overstatement, what makes *Platonov* a real portent of Chekhov's mature work is the unsteady listing from the comic side to the serious. It bespeaks a view of the cohesiveness of life, in which important issues and meaningless trivia co-exist. Chekhov's career as a professional humourist made him alert to the grotesque detail, the absurd facet of any situation; but more important is his ingrained awareness that the current of life, awash with the banal flotsam of everyday, sweeps away heroic poses and epic aspirations. A comic effect is natural when grandiose philosophical questions and emotional crises have to share space with the inexorable demands of the humdrum.

'Ivanov'

Ivanov, Chekhov's first work to be staged, was written at the prompting of Korsh and in the wake of the creative gust that had produced the important transitional story 'The Steppe'. Chekhov dashed off the play in a couple of weeks in October 1887, pleased with its 'unhackneyed subject' and its lack of longueurs. He defined his own originality this way: 'Modern dramatists start their plays exclusively with angels, cads and buffoons – try and find those elements anywhere in Russia! Sure, you'll find them, but not in such extreme guises as dramatists need. I wanted to do something original; I didn't hatch out a single villain, a single angel (although I couldn't refrain from buffoons), I didn't accuse anyone, I didn't acquit anyone' (to Aleksandr, 24 October 1887). He intended to 'sum up everything that's been written so far about whining and languishing people, and in my *Ivanov* to put an end to this writing' (to Suvorin, 7 January 1889). This determination shows *Ivanov* to be not a reconstruction of *Without Patrimony*, but a counterblast to it and its ilk.

Ivanov was first played at Korsh's Theatre in Moscow on 19 November 1887, for the benefit of Nikolay Svetlov who created Borkin; it enjoyed a great success. The actors' praise and the audiences' plaudits made Chekhov euphoric, and he wrote to Aleksandr, 'You can't imagine what's happened! From that insignificant turd that is my playlet . . . the devil knows what has occurred . . . in his 32 years in the theatre the prompter had never seen anything like it'. He triumphantly signed himself, 'Schiller Shakespearovich Goethe' (to Aleksandr, 24 November 1887). But his younger brother Mikhail recalled the event differently. 'The success of the performance was spotty: some hissed, others, the majority, noisily applauded and called for the author, but in general *Ivanov* was not understood, and for a long time afterwards the newspapers were explicating the personality and character of its main hero.' The impressionable playwright gradually came to the conclusion that the audience had welcomed Ivanov himself as a distillation of the *Zeitgeist*. His mooning and moaning, his fits of self-castigation summed up for the generation of the 1880s its own pusillanimous torpor during the 'darkling decade,' a period of political repression and social inaction. His death provided a kind of vicarious expiation.

That was not what Chekhov had in mind. Superficially, Ivanov, his name the Russian equivalent of 'Jones', seemed another common- or garden-variety 'superfluous man,': 'a university graduate, in no way remarkable; a somewhat excitable, ardent nature, strongly inclined to honourable and straightforward enthusiasm, like most educated gentry,' was how Chekhov described him. Like Platonov, his past is nobler than his present; his projects for serving the people, rational farming, higher education have evaporated. But Chekhov wanted to get away from the apotheosis of this disillusionment, by then a stale treatment, to an examination by the character himself of the reasons for his empty life and contemptible behaviour. Ivanov was to suffer through his own awareness of wasted potential and vestigial honour. A basic dramatic problem was to keep the audience from idealising Ivanov's pessimism and, at the same time, to keep Ivanov from looking like the immoralist that Doctor Lvov makes him out to be.

The stage portrayal of this complex inner turmoil was tricky for an inexperienced playwright, trying to employ age-old strategies of dramatic carpentry to contain a richly psychological subject. Basically, the 'plot' might have come from a society melodrama by Dyachenko. A scoundrel abandons his exploited wife in hopes of repairing his fortunes by wedding a young heiress: this sensational story-line is how Ivanov's actions look to outsiders such as Lvov. Ibsen had already managed to sublimate such a triangle into the internalised conflicts of *Rosmersholm*, with the bedevilled intellectual Rosmer torn between coequal calls to duty. Chekhov, however, was constrained to write long expository speeches, endless explanations, confessions, acts of contrition, to counter his audience's preconceptions of heroism and villainy.

The earliest revision was for the Alexandra Theatre in St. Petersburg. Chekhov wrote, 'Now my Mr. Ivanov will be much better understood. The finale doesn't satisfy me exactly (except for the shooting, everything is weak) but I am comforted that its form is still not finished' (19 December 1888). Originally, Ivanov had died on stage of a heart attack and Chekhov realized that this posed a problem for an actor while it undermined the real causes of Ivanov's destruction.

The play's life-blood is gossip. In the first act, we hear of slanderous rumours about Ivanov, but no one takes them too seriously. In the second act, the school for scandal is in session at Lebedev's home, but the gossipmongers are so caricatured that again their power to harm is discounted. Ivanov is now associated with Borkin's shady machinations, however. In Act Three, Lebedev still refuses to believe the tattle, but warns Ivanov, 'There're so many rumours about you running through the county, watch out, our friend the District Attorney may turn up . . . You're a murderer, and a vampire, and a grave-robber . . .' Aided by Lvov, the rumours reach Anna's ears, provoking her confrontation with Ivanov and her collapse. In the play's first version, this theme continued into Act Four, with even Lebedev succumbing to doubts about Anna's death. Ivanov, definitively charged with villainy by the Doctor, dies of a heart attack 'because,' said Chekhov, 'he can't endure the outrageous insult' (letter to Aleksandr, 20 November 1887).

This was to turn the play into a tract about provincial narrowmindedness, and, indeed, many of the critics described Ivanov as the honourable but vacillating victim of scandalmongers. So Chekhov added Sasha to the attackers in Act Four, and had Ivanov taking active measures in his own defence. He gave him a long monologue about dreams of becoming the young Ivanov once more. 'If Ivanov turns out looking like a cad or a superfluous man, and the doctor a great man . . . then, obviously, my play won't come off, and there can be no talk of a production' (to Suvorin, 30 December 1888).

Doctor Lvov therefore needed touching up. In traditional drama, doctors were *raisonneurs*, whose sagacious moralizing clued the audience into the way to think about the characters. But Lvov does not heal breaches: he creates them through his purblind and self-righteous assumptions. In this respect, he much resembles Gregers Werle in Ibsen's *The Wild Duck*, who, in his quixotic attempt to strip away illusions, destroys the lives of those around him. Chekhov's task was to make sure that Lvov did not seem either an objective spokesman or a fatuous prig. 'Such persons are necessary, and for the most part sympathetic. To draw them as caricatures, even in the interests of the stage is dishonorable and serves no purpose' (to Suvorin, 30 December 1888).

Rehearsals for the Petersburg production went badly, despite a strong cast, and Chekhov quarrelled with the comic actor Vladimir Davydov who played the lead in a monotonous style to indicate seriousness. The opening night was a huge success, but Chekhov sneaked away, regarding the ovations as intoxication that would later give him a severe hangover. He continued to revise *Ivanov*, dropping one comic character, Dudkin, and, in general, toning down the farce elements. A third version appeared in 1889, with more explanations added between Lvov and Anna, and the removal of the dream monologue of Ivanov in the last act. Even then, Chekhov was not content and kept touching it up until 1901.

Chekhov never managed to eliminate the mannerisms of boulevard drama that vitiated the subtlety of his concept. The Act Two curtain, with a consumptive wife intruding on her husband in the arms of another woman, is effective claptrap; at least we are spared the fainting which is described in the next act. Scenes of vituperation rise, in the best melodrama manner, to one consummate insult. 'Kike bitch,' Ivanov screams at Anna in his ugliest moment; 'Bastard!' (or 'Cad' 'Villain' – *podlets* is too dated to translate well) is the summation of Lvov's contempt for Ivanov. Chekhov was to handle the slanging-match between Arkadina and Treplyov in *The Seagull* more saliently. Even the final suicide is, as the critic Kugel said, 'a sacrifice made by Chekhov's soul to the god of theatrical gimmickry,'[4] literally ending the play with a bang. It may have been copied directly from Luka Antropov's popular comedy-melodrama *Will-o'-the-Wisps* (1873).

Even toned down, the comic characters are reduced to a series of tics and hardly seem to exist on the same plane as the primary characters. Kosykh is nothing more than his obsession with cards; Zinaida becomes the epitome of her stinginess, 'Madame Gooseberry-Jam'. Gradually, Chekhov learned how to make farcical elements more revelatory of his plays' inner meanings. On the other hand, Shabelsky's off-again-on-again courtship of the widow sardonically comments on Ivanov's own conscience-stricken interest in Sasha. Here the comedy has the Shakespearean function of a reflective subplot, with the result that 'two weddings are spoilt'.

Within the conventional framework, however, a Chekhovian sense of atmospherics is beginning to emerge. He knew well the resonance that derived from a properly-chosen setting, and structured the play to alternate private and public life. We first see Ivanov *solus*, seated in a natural surrounding against the background of his house; he is outside it, because it represents to him a suffocating prison to be escaped. But the primal image of isolated Ivanov is shattered by Borkin with his gun.

As if to exacerbate the incursions into his privacy, Ivanov flees to a more peopled spot, the party at the Lebedevs. But there the guests are already yawning at the very boredom he hoped to avoid. Act Two begins in a crowd of persons, some so anonymous as to be designated only as First Guest, Second Guest, etc.; this chorus makes common knowledge deeds performed in private. Even before Ivanov and Shabelsky appear, their lives are trotted forth as gossip and conjecture; Ivanov's innermost motives are distorted, and his most intimate action here, the embrace of Sasha, is intruded upon by the worst possible witness, his wife.

Act Three returns to Ivanov's study, which ought to be his sanctum, but is, as the stage direction makes clear, a jumble, a visual metaphor for the disorder of his existence. His papers, presumably the products of his brain, lie cheek by jowl with food and drink, brought in by others, who expatiate on gastronomy. Coming as it does after Anna's melodramatic discovery, this interlude strikes the note of triviality, and neutralises what might otherwise be overly theatrical. It is Chekhov's way of cooling overheated actions by pairing them with the banal. Ivanov himself seems aware of this, for he resents the impinging of his workaday fellows on his moping. Their commentary reduces his soul-searching to cheap and obvious motives.

'It's like living in Australia!' says Kosykh, unwittingly evoking this provincial barbarity where vast expanses stretch between estates, and yet privacy is impossible. The last act sanctions a medley of public and private worlds as the wedding party prepares for blessing before going to church. The event could not be more gregarious, despite the personal nature of the conjugal bond, and the characters have difficulty finding a quiet corner in which to unburden their minds. Ivanov's entrance is regarded as tactless invasion, a bridegroom seeing the bride before the ceremony; and his self-destruction is enacted before a crowd of horrified onlookers.

Suicide as a public act chimes in with Ivanov's continual self-dramatisation. He and his uncle Shabelsky put a literary construction on life. The Count tends to compare persons to characters in Gogol, life to events in French plays and novels. Ivanov points the comparisons inward: 'I'm dying of shame that I'm a healthy, strong man, and not turning into Hamlet or Manfred or a superfluous man'. Dr Lvov labels Ivanov a Tartuffe, Molière's classic hypocrite. Most frequent is the Lazarus image, the dead man who might yet be called from the tomb if Sasha acts the Saviour. During the wedding preparations, Ivanov is told not to be a Chatsky, Griboyedeov's comic hero who regarded his society with scorn and was taken by it to be a madman. Ivanov's problem often seems to be an embarrassment of role models, none of which adequately expresses his complexity. Despite the conspectus of opinion that runs from Sasha's hero-worship to the malign slanders of the party-guests, Ivanov's character does not get beyond his own verbose self-scrutiny. 'How can a man see into another man's soul?' he asks Lvov. Chekhov did his best to present the evidence fairly, but he had yet to achieve the proper form.

'The Wood Demon'

In 1888, even before he had finished work on *Ivanov*, Chekhov suggested to Suvorin that they collaborate on a comedy. They drew up a list of characters, episodes and a distribution of assignments. Suvorin soon dropped out, and Chekhov reworked the play into *The Wood Demon* in Spring 1889.

41

'The play turned out boring, pieced together like a mosaic, . . . nowhere in the whole play is there a single lackey or peripheral comic character or little widow. There are eight characters in all and only three of them are episodic. As a rule I tried to avoid superfluity, and I think I have succeeded' (to Suvorin, 14 May 1888).

The Wood Demon was read by the committee that passed on plays for the Petersburg state theatres, whose members included Grigorovich, the critic who had persuaded Chekhov to be a serious writer. Its devastating and unanimous decision was unanimously to reject *The Wood Demon* as 'a beautiful dramatised novella'.[5] However, the play was solicited by Chekhov's boyhood friend Solovtsov, who had left Korsh's to start a new theatre in Moscow with Madam Abramova. So *The Wood Demon*, with a hastily rewritten fourth act, was first presented at Abramova's private theatre on 27 December 1889, in a very weak production. The role of Yelena was taken by the corpulent actress Mariya Glebova, and, as Mikhail Chekhov remembered, 'to see the *jeune premier*, the actor Roshchin-Insarov, making a declaration of love to her was positively incongruous; he called her beautiful, yet he could not get his arms round her to embrace her. Then the glow of the forest fire was such that it raised laughter'.[6] Dissatisfied, Chekhov withdrew the play, which had been at best received with indifference.

But Chekhov's dissatisfactions related more directly to its internal imperfections than to its faulty staging. The problem with *The Wood Demon* is that it tries very hard to make a positive statement. It had been preceded by the novella *A Boring Story*, whose central characters, a played-out scientist and his ward, a despairing actress, have reached an impasse in life. No way out of the sterility that confronts them seems possible. Adverse critics had been dwelling on Chekhov's so-called pessimism, and it was beginning to get under his skin.

During work on *The Wood Demon* Chekhov enunciated his most eloquent statement of political non-alignment:

> I am not a liberal, not a conservative, not a gradualist, not a monk, not an indifferentist. I would like to be an independent artist, except that I'm sorry God hasn't given me the strength to be one. I hate lies and violence in all their guises ... Phariseeism, obtuseness and despotism do not prevail only in merchants' households and lockups, I see them in science, literature, among the young ... Trademarks and labels I consider to be prejudice. My holy of holies is the human body, health, intelligence, talent, inspiration, love and the most absolute freedom. This is the programme I would adhere to if I were a great artist (to A. N. Pleshcheyev, 4 October 1888).

Personal integrity was more important for Chekhov than political adherence; he was no joiner.

Yet he was drawn to the increasingly popular teachings of Tolstoy, even though he rejected such tenets as asceticism and passive resistance to evil. In *The Wood Demon* he subscribes to the Tolstoyan notion of universal love as a means of cutting through the Gordian knot of social problems. The cast of characters he had drawn up for Suvorin had included two Tolstoyan characters: Anuchin, an old man, who as the result of a public repentance became the happiest person in the district, and the pilgrim Fedossy, a plain-speaking and optimistic lay brother of the Mt. Athos monastery. All that survives of these characters in *The Wood Demon* is a last act speech of Orlovsky Senior who relates his mid-life crisis and regeneration. By shouting 'My friends, my good people, forgive me, for the love of Christ!', he has become a paragon of loving-kindness and contentment.

That was the mood Chekhov intended to pervade the play. 'I filled the comedy with good, healthy people, half sympathetic, and a happy ending. The general tone is entirely lyrical' (to Pleshcheyev, 30 September 1889). Like many of Strindberg's late dramas, it is a play of conversion, but without overt religious references or a confessional tone. For the development of Chekhov's playwriting skills, the most important new feature is the suppression of a prominent hero in favour of a closely interrelated group. On this provincial estate the ties that bind the characters are more intricate than those in *Ivanov*.

Attractive young Yelena is married to an old, ailing, famous professor, and feels frustrated. She is wooed by two men: Voynitsky, a sour malcontent who feels he has wasted his life in supporting the Professor, and Fyodor Orlovsky, a rich young wastrel, whose father dotes on him. The professor's daughter by an earlier marriage, Sofiya, is intelligent but drily rationalistic. She is loved by Doctor Khrushchyov, nicknamed the Wood Demon for his work in reforestation and conservation; she returns his affection but they mistrust one another's attitudes. Sofiya is hopelessly courted as well by the young landowner Zheltukhin, whose sister Yuliya has long loved Fyodor Orlovsky from afar, but cannot get him to change his wild ways. This lack of reciprocity and sympathy is, for Chekhov, more than a means of complicating the plot; it sounds the thematic note for the unbearable life these people lead. As Yelena says to Voynitsky, 'Everyone's warring against everyone else. Ask yourself, what's the sense of this war, what's it for?' The situation worsens to the point that Voynitsky shoots himself and Yelena runs away, and it is the task of the fourth act to unravel these misunderstandings and pose a solution.

'The world will be destroyed not by robbers and thieves,' declares Yelena, 'but by covert hatred, the enmity between good people, all these nasty squabbles.' Therefore, these good people must set things right, by casting aside narrow-minded distrust. Krushchyov complains that his neighbours unthinkingly define him as 'a populist, a psychopath, a phrase-monger, – whatever you like, but not a human being!'; and when Sofiya labels him a 'democrat' and a 'Tolstoyan', he explodes, 'That's no way to live! – Whoever I am, look me straight in the eye, clearly, without ulterior motives, without programmes and try to find the human being in me first, or else there'll never be peace in your relations with people'.

Baldly put, this formulates the play's ideology, and the happy ending that Chekhov boasted of comes about as the characters discover this idea for themselves. The couples who had been divided by mutual distrust now link up, and stand on the brink of a new life full of truth.

In the first version of *The Wood Demon*, this was not entirely clear and Chekhov worked hard to remove similarities to *Ivanov*. He radically changed the character of Zheltukhin, whom he had portrayed as a typically liberal, slogan-spouting landowner, prone to quote the populist poet Nekrasov. In Chekhov this is always a sign of insincerity: he later links it with Arkadina in *The Seagull* and the mendicant tramp in *The Cherry Orchard*, and elements of Zheltukhin's phrase-making recur there in Gayev. Sofiya was made to complain that her neighbours were all museum-pieces: 'Populists in embroidered peasant-shirts, district doctors who resemble Bazarov [in *Fathers and Sons*] . . . Tolstoyans who when they pay a call insist on coming through the kitchen or the back way'. Chekhov struck all this out lest he be accused of the very labelling for which he rebukes his characters.

In the produced version, the characters are pretty obviously divided between the self-centred rationalists, (Voynitsky, his mother, Zheltukhin, the Professor and Sofiya before her reformation); and the pure-in-heart, who avoid self-analysis and are direct and open in their reactions (the Orlovskys, Yuliya, Waffles). Chekhov strove hard to change the play's ending in order to point up this schism. Originally, the Professor was to undergo a change of heart, see the error of his ways and forgive Yelena, whereas Fyodor who had carried her off would behave like a hotheaded duellist until he receives news of his father's death. Instead, the naïve Waffles was made to abduct Yelena, and Orlovsky senior did not die of shock. In the final version, it is Fyodor who undergoes a rather sudden and unconvincing conversion to simplicity and sensitivity, while the Professor remains unyielding to the end.

Khrushchyov the Wood-demon[7] lends his name to the play, not because he is the pivotal figure but because his epiphany in the last act is the summation of the play's meaning.

There's a wood-demon lurking in me, I'm petty, untalented, blind, but even you, professor, are no eagle! And at the same time the whole county, all the women see me as a hero, a progressive, and you are famous throughout Russia. Well, if people like me are seriously taken to be heroes and if people like you are seriously famous, that must mean there's a shortage of human beings and every Jack's a gentleman, there are no genuine heroes, no talents, no people who would lead us

out of this darkling wood, who would put right what we
ruin, no real eagles with a right to respect and fame . . .

In Chekhov's later plays, a speech like this would be
alloyed by some ironic flaw in the character; here it is
meant to be taken as read. The critic Chudakov noted that
Khrushchyov is perhaps the first hero in Russian theatre
'whose purpose in life is the preservation of nature,'[8] but
unlike Astrov, his counterpart in *Uncle Vanya*, Khrushchyov's concern with conservation is not, by itself, a
redeeming trait. Merit is not achieved by saving forests or
serving science or by any practical activity; pure morality in
human relations is of higher value. The crucial turning-
point for Khrushchyov is the finding of Voynitsky's diary,
which shows him how wrong he was to slander Yelena. The
device is clumsy, a relic of the well-made play, but Chekhov
needs it to propel Khrushchyov's *volte-face*, his awakening,
when he casts off his suspicions of others.

> I didn't shoot myself and I didn't cast myself into the
> millrace . . . Maybe I'm not a hero, but I shall become
> one! I shall sprout eagle's wings, and won't be frightened
> by this blaze or the devil himself! Let the forest burn – I'll
> plant a new one! Let someone not love me – I'll fall in
> love with someone else!

By means of rhetoric Chekhov is endeavouring to
surpass his earlier dramatic statements. Both *Without
Patrimony* and *Ivanov* centred upon somewhat outstanding individuals corroded by their own cynicism, self-doubt
and reflective propensities. In *The Wood Demon*, those
qualities re-emerge in Voynitsky, who, riddled with
irony, finds the less complicated natures of Fyodor and
Khrushchyov appealing; himself incapable of change, he

has to commit suicide, to leave the stage clear for the reversals of the last act.

Because message is so important in this play, medium is more ungainly than usual with Chekhov. His recourse to such tried-and-true gimmicks as the overheard and misunderstood conversation, the all-explaining document that turns up at the critical moment, the speedy peripeteias that arrive in time to arrange a symmetrical tableau of lovers for the curtain-call made Chekhov himself wince. For at just this period he was hoping to forge a new dramaturgy, to create 'a play where people would arrive, depart, talk about the weather, dine, play cards, but not because that is what goes on in life . . . We don't need realism or naturalism, we don't need to adjust to any sort of frame. We need life to be what it is and people what they are, not on stilts'.[9] He did manage to bring real life on stage in *The Wood Demon*: everyday talk, casually tossed-off phrases, pauses as signs of inner concentration provide the fundamental texture. Such a seemingly minor detail as Yelena's playing Lensky's pre-duel aria from *Yevgeny Onegin* as Act Three starts bears a close relation to what will occur in the act: an explosion of violence between two men, ending in the shooting death of one of them.

Except for that third act, each tableau is grouped around a food-laden table, where the characters' participation in or withdrawal from the communal act of eating has dramatic weight. Yuliya spends the first act of *The Wood Demon* pressing pie and vodka on her guests, Waffles dilates on the virtues of a ham, champagne is ordered. Khrushchyov's hearty appetite is meant to be more attractive than Fyodor's attention to drink. Act Two takes place in the dining-room, and the affinity between Khrushchyov and Sofiya is revealed by their communion in cheese and vodka after hours, as later, she and Yelena will pledge friendship in a glass of wine. The reconciliations and revelations of the last act are staged at a picnic prepared by Waffles. The spoiled Professor is told by no-nonsense Yuliya that she won't add sugar to his tea: 'have your tea with jam'. When Fyodor enters with a hangover, he takes his with 'lemon, as sour as you please'. Yuliya and Waffles insist that he stick to tea and rusks as an emblem of his promised reformation.

Still, the attention to real life could not conceal the play's contrived denouement, tendentiousness and manipulation of psychology. Chekhov refused, despite the pleas of enthusiasts to have it reprinted. 'I hate that play and am trying to forget it,' he wrote later (to A. I. Urusov, 16 April 1900). But the ideology, if too blatantly expressed, was to abide; Chekhov's later plays continued to attribute greater importance to honesty in human relations than to any doctrinaire or programmatic prescriptions for society.

4
The One-Act Plays

'The difference between a full-length play and a one-act is simply quantitative,' Chekhov once remarked (to Suvorin, 14 October 1888). The generic term he used was vaudeville, 'a one-act drama or comedy', but his short plays are not technically *vaudevilles*, since they lack two standard features of that form: intrigue, in the French sense of an articulated plot whose *données* are established at the start, and songs, verses set to familiar tunes that express the characters' intimate feelings. Often Chekhov termed his short comic plays *shutki*, jokes not unlike the squibs he submitted to comic papers in his early days as a writer.

'In one-act pieces, one has to write *nonsense* – therein lies their strength,' he declared. But at the same time, he refused to consider such an activity as frivolous.

Sergeyenko is writing a tragedy on the life of Socrates. These pigheaded boors always latch on to greatness, because they don't know how to create something small and they have disproportionately grandiose pretensions,

50

in default of literary taste. It is easier to write about Socrates than to write about a young girl or a cook. (To Suvorin, 2 January 1894, shortly before starting on *The Seagull*, which has in it both a young girl and a cook.)

His basic formula for a successful farce was compounded of: (a) a complete mix-up; (b) everyone on stage a clear-cut character, speaking his own language; (c) no long drawn-out passages; and (d) uninterrupted action (to A. S. Lazarev, 15 November 1887). Even when Chekhov begins with a hackneyed ploy, he manages to instill fresh vigour into it through well-observed characters, and, perhaps less apparent in translation, juicy dialogue.

Conflicts arise from breakdowns in communication, the misuse of ordinary units of meaning. The device of a business-like conversation going off on a tangent and seldom coming home is a time-honoured one in Russian comic literature: it is practically the underlying principle of Gogol's narrative technique. A character in Gogol's first version of *The Inspector General*, the ancient military man Rastakovsky, rambles on interminably about past campaigns; Chekhov revives the device in the deaf naval officer of *The Wedding*. In Turgenev's hilarious farce, *Luncheon with the Marshal of Nobility*, the obtuse biddy Kaurova repeatedly disrupts a 'peaceable settlement' with her vagaries; Chekhov would make her the model for the harridan Merchutkina in *The Jubilee*.

Almost every one of Chekhov's vaudevilles begins with a hoary stage tradition, a major character explaining at length to the audience his present circumstances. This bald exposition sets the scene for the ensuing complications. Usually two characters of differing temperament work at cross-purposes, their actions accompanied by the commentary of a third, less involved character. *The Bear* and *The*

Proposal derive much of their fun from such an arrangement.

Even in those simple forms, Chekhov was relying on a context that he would exploit more authoritatively in *The Wedding*, *The Jubilee*, and *Tatyana Repina*: a familiar social ritual to set off the satirical point. A period of mourning, a marriage proposal, a wedding ceremony, a nuptial banquet, an anniversary presentation are all relatively formal occasions, whose basic outlines are familiar to every member of a society. Each person knows how he is expected to behave at such times. But in Chekhov's one-acts, under the duress of monomania and personal stress these rituals collapse, revealing the frailty of their shared assumptions. The putative relationships prove to be faulty, the bonds of affection or sympathy wanting. In these shorter works, Chekhov's vaunted objectivity resembles impassivity, and he seems almost cruel to his creatures.

The finales of the farces are, in the earliest works, conventional enough: a wedding in the offing or an invitation to a drink, the standard New Comedy termination. Endings gave Chekhov a hard time:

> I've got an interesting plot (*syuzhet*) for a comedy, but I haven't yet come up with an ending. Whoever invents new endings for plays will open a new era. Trite endings don't work! The hero either gets married or shoots himself, there's no other way out . . . Each act I finish like a story: I carry on the whole act peacefully and quietly, and at the end give the spectator a sock in the jaw (to Suvorin, 4 June 1892).

The development to be traced in his dramatic finales, from the suicides in *Ivanov* and *The Seagull*, the engagements in *The Wood Demon*, to the open-ended continuum of his final masterpieces, is conspicuous in the one-acts as well. Life goes squalidly on in *The Wedding*, life is startled into a frozen tableau in *The Jubilee*. A neat disposition of the characters' fates is no longer possible.

'On The Highway'

Chekhov wrote this 'dramatic étude' – which he privately referred to as a 'little nonsense for the stage' in autumn 1884. The piece was based on a short story 'Autumn' that had appeared the previous year. Story and play share the same locale, Uncle Tikhon's pothouse, and the same basic premise: a nobleman on the skids gives the tavernkeeper a medallion with the portrait of his unfaithful but still loved wife, to pay for another tot of vodka. A peasant who used to be in his service recognizes the gentleman and relates his unhappy history.

Adapting this for the stage, Chekhov conscientiously enlarged his canvas. The anonymous 'company of cabmen and pilgrims' is differentiated into the pilgrims Nazarovna and Yefimovna, the religious itinerant Savva, and the factory worker Fedya. But the valuable new astringent in the dramatic blend is the tramp Yegor Merik, who had also suffered an unhappy love affair in the past. Unfortunately, Chekhov felt that his prose sketch was too static as it stood, and so he had recourse to a violent climax. The gentleman's wife, by the most unlikely of coincidences, takes shelter in the pothouse and is almost killed by the delirious Merik. The story had ended with the author's rhetorical question, 'Spring, where art thou?' The play concludes with Merik's overwrought exclamation, 'My anguish! My vicious anguish! Pity me, orthodox folk!'

The play was submitted to the censor, an unavoidable step if it was to be performed on a public stage. This particular censor, who bore the burlesque name of E. I. Kaiser-von-Nilckheim, indignantly underlined the word 'gentleman' (*barin*) every time it appeared in the manuscript, and in his unfavourable report, commented that 'among all the vagrants and transients come to the pot-house to get warm and spend the night, there appears a decayed *aristocrat* (*dyoryanin*) who *prays the tapster to give him a drink on credit* . . . This gloomy and squalid play, in my opinion, cannot be allowed for production.'[1] Kaiser-von-Nilckheim has thus the dubious distinction of being the first of a long string of critics to complain that Chekhov's plays are gloomy.

The play was not published until 1914, ten years after Chekhov's death, when a production was mounted at the Malakhov Theatre in Moscow. Reviewers varied in their assessments from ecstatic – one of them saw Fedya as an archetype of Lopakhin in *The Cherry Orchard* – to, mostly, hostile. Used to the lyrical qualities of Chekhov's mature works, they were appalled by the raw melodrama of *On the Highway*.

'On The Harmfulness of Tobacco'

Originally, Chekhov intended this as a monologue for the talented though alcoholic comedian Gradov-Sokolov, and dashed it off in two and a half hours in February, 1886. He spent the rest of his career returning to it, revising and emending it, until it reached the shape in which it is ordinarily reprinted today. Six distinct variants exist, the more serious changes concomitant with the greater depth of psychology of Chekhov's works throughout the 1890s. Over the course of this recension, Chekhov heightened the emotional tone of the monologue, refined the comedy and increased the pathos. The speaker's pseudo-scientific jargon became more attenuated, with a concurrent introduction of clichés.

Nyukhin (the name suggests sniffing snuff, the perfect comic tag for a lecturer on the evils of tobacco) has been forced by his wife to deliver a lecture. During this half-hearted address, he reveals his henpecked existence and his insignificance in the life of his family. As draft followed draft, Nyukhin began to cast more aspersions on his unseen wife and to reveal more hatred for his enforced nullity. What Chekhov had earlier left the audience to deduce was now spelled out in tones of complaint. The pure ridicule that had been showered on his hero was turned to pity, and Nyukhin became the latest in the Russian tradition of the put-upon 'little man'.

'Swan Song' (Calchas)

Chekhov based *Calchas* (late 1886 or early 1887) on a short story of the same name; like the previous play, it was meant as a 'dramatic étude' for a popular comic actor, Davydov. 'It should play 15 to 20 minutes,' Chekhov suggested. 'As a rule little things are much better to write than big ones: they're less pretentious, but still successful . . . what more does anyone need?' (to M. V. Kiseleva, 14 January 1887). Davydov performed it at Korsh's Theatre on 19 February 1888, but put in so many ad-libs about great actors of the past that Chekhov could barely recognize his script. Later he made some slight emendations which he submitted to the censorship in hopes of a performance in a State theatre, and changed the title to *Swan Song*. 'A long title, bitter-sweet, but I can't think up another, although I thought a long time' (to Lensky, 26 October 1888). (It's six syllables in Russian: *Lebedinaya pesna*.)

Svetlovidov – which means 'of bright aspect', probably a *nom de théâtre* – has, like one of Tolstoy's heroes, begun life as an army officer but lost caste by going on the stage. Even there, his career has been one of decline, from tragedian to buffo. He has been playing Calchas, the wily old oracle-monger in Offenbach's comic opera *La Belle Hélène*, a secondary part chosen for his benefit, no doubt because the popular operetta would fill the house. Its standard costume consisted of a short Attic tunic and tights on his 68-year old legs. So, throughout this play, Svetlovidov's declamation from *King Lear*, *Othello* and *Hamlet* is continually contradicted by his ludicrous appearance.

Although the play draws heavily on Dumas' *Kean* to allow a skilled character actor a field-day, it still encompasses a serious Chekhovian theme – coming to terms with life. Svetlovidov, in the course of fifteen minutes, passes from self-aggrandisement as a ruined tragedian to self-contempt as a hammy clown to self-acceptance as an attendant lord, like T. S. Eliot's Prufrock, who can 'swell a progress, start a scene or two'. At the height of his delusion, he spouts Lear's storm speech; but by the end, he exits with a pettish repudiation of society from Griboyedov's classic comedy *Woe From Wit*. This *diminuendo* hints at a pocket enlightenment, a compressed version of the awareness that tragic heroes take five acts to achieve.

'The Bear'

As usual, Chekhov's earliest reference to his work-in-progress was offhandedly negative: 'Having nothing to do, I wrote a vapid little Frenchy vaudevillette (*vodevil chik*) entitled *The Bear*' (to I. L. Leontiev-Shcheglov, 22 February 1888). No sooner had it appeared in print, than Chekhov's friends insisted that he submit it to the censor and recommended the perfect actors to play it. The censor was not amused, disturbed by the 'more than strange plot,' 'the coarseness and indecency of the tone of the whole play,'[2] and forbade production. But he was overruled by a superior bureaucrat who, by suppressing a few lines, rendered it suitable for the public. It had its première at Korsh's on 28 October 1888, with the clever ingenue Nataliya Rybchinskaya as Popova and Chekhov's boyhood friend Nikolay Solovtsov as Smirnov. Solovtsov, a tall, ungainly fellow with a huge voice, had probably been in Chekhov's mind for the role of the bear as he wrote it.

The Bear was, from the start, a runaway success: the audience roared with laughter and interrupted the dialogue with applause, and the newspapers praised it to the skies. Theatres all over Russia added it to their repertoires and the best Russian actors clamoured to play in it. In Chekhov's lifetime it brought him in regular royalties and has held the stage throughout the Soviet era.

The Bear's comedy proceeds from the characters' lack of self-knowledge: the widow Popova fancies herself inconsolably bereaved, a fugitive from the world, while Smirnov takes himself to be a misogynist to the core. It updates Petronius' ancient tale of the Widow of Ephesus, which Christopher Fry later turned into *A Phoenix Too Frequent.* That ribald fable tells of a widow whose grief for a dead husband melts under the ardour of the soldier guarding a crucified corpse; she eventually colludes with him to substitute her own deceased spouse for the body stolen during their love-making. Chekhov puts the pony Toby in place of the corpse, as a token of the transference of the widow's affection; he also doubles the comic reversal.

Both Popova and Smirnov are *alazons* in the classic sense: figures made comic by pretending to be more than they actually are. If the languishing Popova derives from the Petronian source, Smirnov is a descendant of Molière's Alceste, professing a hatred of society's hypocrisy but succumbing to a woman who exemplifies that society. The two poseurs come in conflict, and the roles reverse: the grieving relict snatches up a pistol and, like any case-hardened bully, insists on a duel while the gruff woman-hater finds himself incapable of facing down his female opponent. (It was the improbable duel that most outraged the critics.) It is in the cards that the frail widow and the brute in muddy boots will fall into one another's arms by the final curtain.

'The Proposal'

'A vulgarish and boringish vaudevillette, but suitable for the provinces' was how Chekhov disparaged *The Proposal*, even while he asked friends to intercede with the censors on its behalf. Inspired by the success of *The Bear*, he was anxious to get his next farce on the boards. It had its first production at the Krasnoe Selo Theatre on 9 August 1889, with a cast of Pavel Svobodin (who had created Shabelsky) as Lomov, Mariya Ilinskaya as Nataliya and the great comic actor Varlamov as Chubukov. It was greeted with unbroken laughter, not least from the Tsar who congratulated the actors. *The Proposal* shared *The Bear*'s fate as a favourite curtain-raiser and benefit play in the provinces for years.

Botched proposals are a Chekhov specialty. The cross-purposes of the 'imaginary invalid' Lomov, incongruously decked out in tails and gloves, and Nataliya in her apron, mount to a boisterous, breathless pitch here. Chekhov understood how to accelerate the basic misapprehensions into a barrage of insults, and how, after building to a climax, to reinvigorate the action by introducing a fresh contretemps (which he may have learned from Turgenev's *Luncheon with the Marshal*). Later, the final interview of Tusenbach and Irina in *Three Sisters*, and Lopakhin's failure to propose to Varya in *The Cherry Orchard* will show Chekhov modulating the tone to one of shattered hopes and mutually conflicting illusions.

'Tatyana Repina'

Tatyana Repina is an anomaly among Chekhov's one-acts: it can be understood only in relationship to another play by someone else. In 1889, Suvorin wrote a 'comedy' founded on an actual occurrence: the suicide eight years earlier of the young actress Yevlaliya Kadmina. Jilted by her lover, she poisoned herself and came on in the last act of Ostrovsky's *Vasilisa Melentieva*, whose heroine is also supposed to die of poison. Kadmina perished in gruesome torments before the eyes of a Kharkov audience, and thus won posthumous notoriety. Chekhov considered her an 'extraordinary celebrity' and even solicited her photograph.

Suvorin's *Tatyana Repina* follows the facts fairly closely. Tatyana Repina, a high-spirited and talented provincial actress, is thrown over by her lover who hopes to repair his ruined fortunes by marrying an heiress. Deeply hurt, publicly insulted by a gross Jewish financier, seeing nothing to live for, Tatyana takes poison before going on stage and dies during the last act of Ostrovsky's play as her friends look on, aghast. From a modern standpoint, Chekhov's enthusiasm for this sensationalist play is hard to comprehend; yet he was lavish with his praise and offered copious advice in his letters. He predicted a success that came to pass in both capitals, and got embroiled in the Moscow rehearsals as an intercessor between actors and

Anton Chekhov

author, when Suvorin was busy staging Chekhov's *Ivanov* in Petersburg.

Chekhov's one-act is therefore a kind of private joke, the 'what happens after the curtain goes down,' that St. John Hankin perfected in his *Dramatic Sequels*. Chekhov purports to be amused by the epidemic of suicides that followed in the wake of *Tatyana Repina*'s success, and he depicts the marriage taking place between the dead actress's lover and his rich heiress. The hieratic formality of the Orthodox wedding ceremony reproduced with considerable authenticity, blended with the trivial remarks of the bystanders, provides the structure. The counterpoint between the sonorous Church Slavonic with its portentous vows and the mundane chitchat of the wedding party produces a sour and sardonic effect. Eventually, the church choir has to compete with a worldly chorus of 'Voices' who begin to spread the news of the suicide epidemic, passing along fragments of tattle. Neurotic females are condemned for this copy-cat *felo de se* at the same time the choir is intoning its 'Lord have mercys' and 'Amens'.

Gradually, the bridegroom's bad conscience overwhelms him and he begins to imagine that Tatyana is there beside him in the church, while her colleagues from the theatre pray for her soul's rest and make disdainful comments about her seducer. When the wedding party finally departs, the remaining clergymen are startled by a woman in black who staggers out from behind a column; she has poisoned herself *à la* Repina and incoherently wavers between fatalism and the desire to be saved.

LADY IN BLACK: . . . Everybody ought to take poison . . . (*Groans and rolls on the floor.*) She's in her grave, while he . . . he . . . To offend a woman is to offend God . . . A woman has perished . . .

FATHER IVAN: What blasphemy against religion! (*Flinging up his arms.*) What blasphemy against life!

LADY IN BLACK (*tears at herself and screams*): Save me! Save me! Save me! . . .

CURTAIN

and the rest I leave to A. S. Suvorin's imagination.

Suvorin's *Tatyana Repina* is interesting for foreshadowing *The Seagull*. Chekhov's favourite character in Suvorin's play was the journalist Adashev, who denigrates his profession as a man of letters in a manner which Chekhov replicated in the Trigorin–Nina interview in *The Seagull*. It is Adashev, a *raisonneur*, who tells Tatyana, after she has, unbeknownst to him, already taken poison, his opinion that suicide is cowardice.

Among us suicide has really become something epidemic. There's no shortage of gunpowder for good people. Children rush for the revolver when they get low grades, grown-ups on account of trifles . . . They fall out of love – a bullet through the brain. Their vanity's been bruised, they aren't appreciated – they shoot themselves. What's happened to strength of character?[3]

Chekhov picks up this notion and carries it to its logical conclusion; he also carries it into his later works. Treplyov's suicide at the end of *The Seagull* and Uncle Vanya's abstraction of morphine must be viewed in this light. After *Ivanov*, Chekhov treated suicide as an act of weakness, an unwillingness to cope with life's demands.

Nina in *The Seagull* is a development of the Tatyana Repina model. In Suvorin's play, the young actress, forlorn in a suburban pleasure garden, hears her ex-lover singing at his bachelor supper.

TATYANA: He? Wait ... Yes, yes, that's his voice ...
l'amour qui nous ... It's he, he ... (*Listens intently.*)[4]

This is Tatyana's lowest ebb, the decisive factor in her
self-destruction. In the last act of *The Seagull*, Nina
overhears the laughter of Trigorin in the dining-room, runs
to the door and states, 'He's here too ... Why, yes ...
Never mind ... Yes'. But Nina's confrontation with this
spectre of her past confirms her in her decision to jettison
the persona of the seagull.

Chekhov's *Tatyana Repina* however, a pastiche not a
parody, is most intriguing as an experiment in polyphonic
structure; in miniature, it practices the intricate interweav-
ing of melodramatic pathos and crass diurnalism that was to
become the trademark of Chekhov's major plays. Not just
the suicides, but the mismatched marriages, failed careers
and dashed hopes that will, in the last plays, be jumbled
amid meals, card-games and dirty galoshes are adumbrated
here. *Tatyana Repina* is a quintessence of Chekhov's notion
of stage naturalism: not a slice of life copied from reality,
but a reconstitution of the casual interconnections that
tangle lives together.

'A Tragedian In Spite Of Himself'

Chekhov had promised Varlamov another acting vehicle
and turned to his story *One of Many* (1887) about a
paterfamilias who must spend his time shunting back and
forth between the dacha where his nearest and dearest are
summering and the town where he carries out their
innumerable commissions. For the sake of the stage,
Chekhov altered the list of errands, deleting among other
items 'a child's coffin', and racy remarks that could pass in
print but would never get past the dramatic censor.

Varlamov did not in fact appear in the play, so that the first actor to create the harried family man was M. I. Bibikov at an amateur performance at the Petersburg German Club on 1 October 1889. Basically, *A Tragedian* remains a comic monologue, with the officious friend acting as straight man.

The allusion to Molière in the title alerts one to the extreme contradictions of the protagonist Tolkachov. Described as 'the father of a family' he begins the play by calling for a pistol to commit suicide and ends it by quoting *Othello*, demanding the blood of his interlocutor. Between these two poles, the banal situation he describes comes less from the world of tragedy than that of existential absurdity. His multifarious errands require him to live in a muddle of inanimate objects. 'For instance, how are you going to lump together a heavy copper mortar and pestle with a lamp-globe or carbolic acid with tea? How are you going to combine beer bottles and this velocipede?' This surrealistic mélange, followed by a detailed comparison of married life with the Israelites' labour in the Egyptian brickyards and the Spanish Inquisition, creates a manic impression of an ordinary middle-class existence as Bosch's hell. Although firmly in the Gogol tradition, Chekhov here moves halfway to Jarry and Ionesco.

'The Wedding'

Chekhov characterised *The Wedding* as 'a scene in one act,' thus distinguishing it from his other short comedies; it differs too in being based on real experiences and individuals in Chekhov's past. The Greek confectioner Dymba was modelled on a clerk in his father's grocery store in Taganrog; the flirtatious midwife he had met when acting as best man at a wedding in 1887. Between 1885 and 1886 he had lived in a Moscow flat beneath the quarters of a caterer who rented our rooms for weddings and balls. At times, he seemed obsessed with weddings, which are the subject of many of his stories written in the 1880s. The one-act was first played at the Art and Literary Society at the Moscow Hunt Club on 28 November 1900, as part of a Chekhov evening; Tolstoy, who was there, laughed till he cried.

The Wedding is a masterful exhibition of the dissolution of social convention. Every pretence kept up by one character is demolished by another; no one's secrets are safe. Over the course of the play, we discover that the groom has married the bride for the sake of a paltry dowry, which has yet to be paid; that the bride herself is totally insensitive to her situation; that her parents are the most narrow and parsimonious of philistines; and that the guests bear no particular good will to the happy pair. The play revolves around one principal deception: to dress out the banquet, a 'General,' that is, a high-ranking official, is required as guest of honour. The bride's mother has charged a friend with this task; he has pocketed the money and brought a deaf naval captain, who assumes that he has been invited. The mother discovers the swindle and turns the old man out without further ado. At that moment, the farcical tone of the play disappears. The old captain, disabused and stripped of any consideration, can only gasp in horror, 'What a shabby trick! What a shabby trick!' After the old man's exit, the guests and hosts revert to their squabbling. The moment of genuine feeling has made no dent in their thick hides.

Again, Chekhov employed the comic device of the gap between the characters' aspirations and reality. Hoping to sound refined, they mangle French and mispronounce polysyllabic words. Zmeyukina, a midwife whose profession is of the earthiest, constantly demands 'atmosphere' and

delicate feeling; she quotes Lermontov in anticipation of
Solyony in *Three Sisters*. The bride's father invariably
dismisses anything unfamiliar with contempt, branding it
'monkey business.' The main oration of the evening is
delivered by a Greek who cannot speak Russian:

> DYMBA (*rises, bashful*). I talk sometings, is no? . . . Is
> Russia. And is Greece. Now in Russia is such a
> peoples, and in Greece is such a peoples . . . And
> peoples on ocean is sailing sheeps, in Russian means
> boots, but on land runs all sorts wildroot drains. I
> understanding good, is no?

Yet when a Russian does rise to speak, it is the Captain,
whose naval lingo is every bit as incomprehensible; assum-
ing that he is entertaining the company, the old salt bores
the guests into stupor and then mutiny. Over the entire
action hangs a sense of affectlessness, no character ever
making true contact with any other. Relatively realistic as it
is, *The Wedding* subjects the lower-middle-class to the
merciless derision of a Daumier.

'The Jubilee'

Private commercial banks were a relatively new feature in
Russian life; the State bank itself dated back only to the
reforms of 1866. The financial institution in Chekhov's
farce is about to celebrate its fifteenth birthday, on which
occasion the bank manager Shipuchin will receive a gift
from grateful shareholders. While he prepares a speech of
thanks and his clerk Khirin is, with an ill will, drawing up
statistics, their work is interrupted by Shipuchin's giddy and
garrulous wife and old Mrs Merchutkina nagging on behalf
of her civil servant husband. The more the women talk, the

65

more the men are driven to distraction. The deputation arrives with its testimonial scroll and silver tankard to behold a vision of chaos: the manager's wife fainting on the sofa, the old lady collapsing in the arms of a babbling Shipuchin, and Khirin threatening the females with murder.

The peculiar position of *The Jubilee* lies halfway between the unsuccessful experiment of *The Wood Demon* and Chekhov's transitional play *The Seagull*. Once again founded on a published short story, *A Defenceless Creature* (1887), it was written in December 1891, but not performed until the Chekhov evening at the Moscow Hunt Club in 1900. By the time *The Jubilee* reached the stage, Chekhov was already known to the general public as the author of *The Seagull, Uncle Vanya*, and *Three Sisters*; many were upset by what seemed a throwback to comic anarchy. The *Moscow News* referred to it as 'a strange play' that ended with 'the bank manager making an insulting gesture at his bookkeeper, while the latter tears books and files to pieces, tossing the ravaged pages in the manager's face.'[5] Chekhov was later to transform this finale to the Gogolian tableau that greets the astonished delegation of stockholders.

The first St. Petersburg production on the stage of the Alexandra in May 1903 was even more questionably received. Although the audience was dying with laughter at the antics of Varlamov as Khirin and the hilarious comedienne Levkeyeva as Merchutkina, certain critics wondered at the crude vulgarity of it all, and speculated whether such a piece had a place in a national theatre. They could not reconcile its extravagant humour with the Checkhov they had grown to expect.

There is a savagery to *The Jubilee* that exceeds even the contumely of *The Wedding*. Each member of the comic quartet is despicable: both women are portrayed as idiotic chatterboxes, the clerk is a crabbed misogynist, and the bank manager Shipuchin an ineffectual ass. The setting enforces hypocrisy: as Shipuchin says, 'At home I can be a philistine and a parvenu and indulge my own little habits, but here everything has to be on a grand scale. This is a bank!' The impending ceremony creates a temporal pressure that propels the mounting hysteria. The result is Homeric laughter, not at all what the textbooks call 'Chekhovian.'

'The Night Before The Trial'

In 1886, Chekhov had published a story by that title, and he returned to it in the early 1890s to convert it into a play. In the process, he intensified the guilt of the main character Zaytsev, causing him to come to trial not simply for bigamy and a series of beatings, but for bigamy, forging his grandmother's will and attempted murder. The scene in which he plays mock doctor to 'examine' the woman in the room next door was considerably enlarged; so was his sleazy courtship of her, and her own character was darkened to make her seem an experienced coquette ready to cuckold her husband. But, because the play was left unfinished, Zaytsev's farewell the next morning and his payment for his 'honest labour' were never worked out, nor was the climax, the scene in court when Zaytsev is surprised to find that the Public Prosecutor is in fact the deceived husband.

Why Chekhov gave it up is a matter for speculation. Perhaps he realised that the seduction would be hard to get past the censorship or that the necessary division into two or three scenes would defeat the comedy's economy as a curtain-raiser. As it stands, *Night Before the Trial* is close to

French boulevard farce in its sexual emphasis. The tone is more insistently vulgar than in any of Chekhov's short plays other than *The Wedding*; bedbugs and fleas are omnipresent, a dramatic legacy from Gogol, no doubt, but emphasised here *ad nauseam*. The mock doctor's examination could easily coarsen into an American burlesque sketch. The Aesopic names Gusev and Zaystev (Goose and Hare) suggest a clown show, and the 'gags' are part of a long popular tradition. Zaytsev (who may in fact be guilty of the crimes he is charged with) contemplates suicide if the verdict goes against him.

> In case the jury finds against me, I'll turn to my old friend . . . A loyal, trusty friend! (*Tales a large pistol from his suitcase*.) here he is! How's the boy? I traded Cheprakov a couple of dogs for him. What a beauty! Just shooting yourself with him would be a kind of satisfaction . . . (*Tenderly*.) You loaded, boy? (*In a piping voice, as if answering for the pistol*.) I'm loaded . . . (*In his own voice*.) I'll bet you'll go off with a bang, right? A real rip-roaring ear-splitter? (*Piping*.) A real rip-roaring ear-splitter . . . (*In his own voice*.) Oh, you silly little thing, gun o'my heart . . . All right, now lie down and go to sleep . . . (*Kisses the pistol and places it in the suitcase*.) As soon as I hear 'Guilty as charged,' then right away – bang to the brain and the sweet bye-and-bye . . .

This ventriloqual exchange as he croons endearments to his suicide weapon is a comic device that goes back at least as far as the *commedia dell'arte* and the folk comedies of Ruzzante. Zaytsev turns into an updated Harlequin, amoral and appetitive, whose ruminations on self-destruction reflect satirically on the suicides in Chekhov's serious works.

Did Chekhov, as he refined his full-length plays and purged them of the grossness of contemporary melodrama and farce, relegate his more exuberant and ironical spirits to the one-act form? The increasing grotesquerie of the series that begins with *Tatyana Repina* certainly suggests it.

5
'The Seagull'

I asked what was most requisite to make a piece fit for the theatre.
  'It must by symbolical,' replied Goethe; 'that is to say, that each incident must be significant by itself, and yet lead naturally to something more important.' *Eckermann's* **Conversations with Goethe** *(26 July 1826)*

Baldly put, the plot of *The Seagull* has the makings of a conventional romance. Arkadina, a flashy and egocentric actress, carrying on a liaison with a famous writer, has a neglected son, who wants to make a name for himself in literature. In his first effort, a play of symbolist tendency, he has featured a naïve and beautiful girl, who longs for fame. But the young man meets with failure in every direction: his play is scoffed at by his mother; the girl, whom he claims to love, becomes infatuated with the famous writer and runs off with him to Moscow; the youth is unable to leave his uncle's estate because his mother will not give him any money and he attempts to take his life, without success. Two years later, all the characters return

70

to the same place: her affair with the writer long over, the girl, Nina, has become a provincial actress, reduced to playing one-night stands in backward county towns. The young man, Treplyov, is now a published writer, his work appearing in the same journal as that of his mother's lover, Trigorin. Masha, the daughter of the estate's overseer, still carries a torch for the young writer, but he ignores her. While the other characters are at supper offstage, Nina and Treplyov have a final interview. Despite his pleas, Nina leaves to pursue her career; frustrated and confused, Treplyov destroys his manuscripts and shoots himself, this time successfully. Any actor, confronted with this scenario, might be excused for falling into standard patterns of characterisation.

The first production of the *The Seagull* at the Alexandra Theatre in St. Petersburg on 17 October 1896 has come down in theatrical legend as a classic fiasco. But this is an exaggeration. The cast was strong, with Davydov (the original Ivanov) as the uncle Sorin, the popular comedian Varlamov (who had already played Lebedev in *Ivanov* and Chubukov in *The Proposal*) as the overseer Shamrayev, the handsome *jeune premier* Roman Apollonsky as Treplyov, and the brilliant young actress Vera Komissarzhevskaya as Nina. During the scant week of rehearsals, Chekhov was in attendance, prompting the actors and correcting the director. Like most sensitive playwrights, he was dismayed by wasted rehearsal time and the actors' predilection for superficial characterisations that stunted his brainchildren; but by the last rehearsals his expectations had risen.

These expectations were dashed on opening night, for the spectators had come with expectations of their own, hoping to see their favorite comedienne Levkeyeva, whose benefit it was. They laughed, booed and whistled at whatever struck them as funny, from Nina's soliloquy to

Treplyov's entrance with the dead gull to the actors' ad-libs when they went up in their lines. Chekhov fled the theatre, vowing never again to write for the stage. Nevertheless, the ensuing performances, with the actors more secure, played to respectful houses. Before *The Seagull* closed in early November, it had become a *succès d'estime*, with Kommissarzhevskaya proclaimed as luminous. It was successfully revived in Kiev, Taganrog and other provincial centres, providing Chekhov with handsome royalties.

Nemirovich-Danchenko, an admirer of the play, thought *The Seagull* just the thing to rescue the flagging fortunes of his newly founded Moscow Art Theatre, whose first season was in danger of bankruptcy. He pressed it upon his reluctant colleague Stanislavsky, who at first found the play incomprehensible and unsympathetic. He retired to his country estate to compose a directorial score which he sent piecemeal to Moscow where Nemirovich rehearsed the actors, including the future director Vsevolod Meyerhold as Treplyov, Olga Knipper, Chekhov's wife-to-be, as Arkadina, and Aleksandr Vishnevsky, the author's boyhood friend, as Dorn. Stanislavsky assumed the role of Trigorin.

Stanislavsky's fundamental approach to staging *The Seagull* differed little from his direction of historical drama. He sought in contemporary Russian life the same picturesque groupings, the same telling mannerisms, the same pregnant pauses that had enthralled audiences when he reconstructed seventeenth-century Muscovy or Renaissance Venice. Rather than inquiring into Chekhov's meaning, Stanislavsky took the play as a romantic melodrama: Nina was an innocent ruined by that 'scoundrelly Lovelace'[1] Trigorin, and Treplyov was a misunderstood Byronic genius, the hero of the piece. Nor, at this stage of his development, did Stanislavsky try organically to elicit performances from the actors. Their every action, reaction and intonation were prescribed by his score and learned by rote.

The opening night, 17th December 1898, despite off-stage jitters was a palpable hit, insuring the theatre's success, and the seagull became the Moscow Art Theatre's trademark. Chekhov was less than ecstatic. He thought that Stanislavsky misinterpreted Trigorin by making him too elegant and formal; he detested Roksanova's Nina. Whatever his misgivings, the middle-class professional audiences took to it precisely because, for the first time, 'the way we live now' was subjected to the same careful counterfeit presentment that had hitherto been applied only to the picturesque past. The spectators beheld their own tics and heard their own speech patterns meticulously copied.

Taking advantage of the outdoor settings of the early acts and the dimly lit interior at the end, Stanislavsky laid on climatic and atmospheric effects to create an overpowering *nastroenie* or mood. The method, relying on sound efects, diffused lighting and a snail's pace, worked so well for *The Seagull* that it became standard operating procedure at the Moscow Art Theatre for Chekhov's later plays and, indeed, those of almost any author. But already astute observers were noting these as obtrusive mannerisms. Prince Urusov, a fan of the Moscow Art Theatre production, called the red lighting at the beginning of Acts One and Four 'completely phoney' and 'unnatural'; 'such lighting, dim and sinister, keeps one from seeing and hearing'. The clever directorial trick of arranging the characters in a row with their backs to the audience 'may be innovative and daring, but ... the actors hunch together embarrassed, compelled to speak to one side, twisting themselves into profiles, – otherwise they can't be heard'.[2]

In the last analysis, it was the mood that permeated that

made *The Seagull* a hit. Meyerhold, in later years, credited Stanislavsky with being the first to link the sound of rain on the window and morning light peeping through the shutters with the characters' behaviour. 'At the time this was a discovery.'[3] The dramatist Leonid Andreyev was to call it 'panpsychology,'[4] the animation of everything in a Chekhov play from distant music to the chirp of a cricket to munching an apple, each sharing an equivalent relation to the play's total effect.

Chekhov's objections to the Moscow interpretation did not, however, spring from its style, but from the imbalance in meaning that Stanislavsky had induced. Although it contains a 'ton of love', *The Seagull* is not a soap opera about a triangular relationship or a romantic dramatisation of Trigorin's 'subject for a short story'. It is perhaps Chekhov's most personal play in its treatment of the artist's *métier*. The theme of splendours and miseries of artists is plainly struck by Nina at the start, when she explains why her parents won't let her come to Sorin's estate: 'They say this place is Bohemia'. Years of theatre-going, reviewing, dealing with performers and managers were distilled by Chekhov to create a density of metaphor for the artistic experience, for the contrasts between commercialism and idealism, facility and aspiration, purposeless talent and diligent mediocrity. Of the central characters, one is an aspiring playwright, another a successful and performed writer; one is an acclaimed star of the footlights, another a would-be actress.

Stanislavsky's black-and-white vision of the play also ran counter to Chekhov's attempt to create multiple heroes and multiple conflicts. Treplyov seems the protagonist because the play begins with his artistic credo and his moment of revolt, and it ends with his self-destruction. But in terms of stage time, he shares the limelight with many other claimants, whose ambitions cancel out one another.

Nor can Nina be singled out as the one survivor who preserves her ideals in spite of all. The type of the victimised young girl, abandoned by her love and coming to a bad end, frequently recurred in Russian literature from Karamzin's *Poor Liza* (1792) onward. Often she was depicted as the ward of an older woman who, in her cruelty or wilful egoism, promotes the girl's downfall: many plays of Ostrovsky and Potekhin feature such a pair, the relationship is subtly handled by Turgenev in *A Month in the Country* (1850). In *The Seagull*, the relationship is rarefied: it is Arkadina's example rather than her intention that sends Nina to Moscow, maternity and mumming.

The pure-souled, lone, provincial actress, a prey to the jealousy of colleagues, the importunities of admirers, and the scorn of society, was an early avatar of the Poor Liza type. In Pisemsky's *One Thousand Souls* (1858) Nastenka, a local girl betrayed, returns to her home town as a famous tragedienne to enjoy a bittersweet reunion with her former lover. This interview parallels the similar scene between Treplyov and Nina. When Nastenka relates her past sufferings and berates her love for not going on with his writing, he flies into a rage and looks to her to save him from himself, which she does. Significantly, Nina does not marry her former suitor out of a sense of duty and fond memories; she sees her duty is to her career, and her memories of 'a bright, warm, joyous, pure life . . . feelings like tender, fragile flowers' are inaccurate. At Nina's most intense moment of recollection, she runs away, leaving the failed writer to save himself, if he can.

Other literary prototypes for Nina include Anninka and Lyubinka in Saltykov-Shchedrin's novel *The Golovlyov Family* (1876), who flee the stifling family estate and after a brief stint in Moscow, descend to touring seedy provincial theatres in musical comedy: seduction, arrest, alcoholism and attempted suicide follow in quick succession. Negina, in Ostrovsky's comedy *Talents and Admirers* (1881), on the other hand, a gifted provincial leading lady, turns down the love of the idealistic student Melusov to go to Moscow with a wealthy landowner in order to further her career.

> MELUSOV: Oh, Sasha, how can you! Are talent and depravity inseparable?
> NEGINA: No, no! Not depravity! Ah, what a man you are . . . understand . . . I'm an actress! But according to you I ought to be some sort of heroine. Yet how can every woman be a heroine? I'm an actress . . . And if I were to marry you I'd soon throw you over and go back to the stage. Even for the smallest salary. Just to be there – on the stage. I can't live without the theatre.[5]

Nina's beginnings, her debut outside Moscow at a summer theatre, her subsequent touring, her dead baby and empty affair, recall the swift decline of Anninka and Lyubinka, as do her third-class railway trips to boom towns like Yelets where 'businessmen with a taste for the arts will pester me with their attentions. A sordid life'. But, like Negina, her faith in her vocation keeps her from succumbing to despair. We even hear Negina's assertion in Nina's 'I'm a gull . . . Not so, I'm an actress. Why, yes!'

Chekhov's early stories abound with actresses who lead erratic lives and endure slurs and contempt for it; but Nina continues to dismiss the shoddiness of the work she is given, determined to develop an inner strength, regardless of old forms or new. Should she be extolled as a shining talent to be contrasted with Arkadina's *routinier* activity? Nina's ideas on art and fame are jejune and couched in the bromides of cheap fiction; her inability to see anything in

Treplyov's play other than words and speeches, her offer to eat black bread and live in a garret for the reward of celebrity, are obtuse and juvenile. Hers are not dreams that deserve to be realised, and there is nothing tragic in her having to reconcile them with the ordinary demands of life.

Similarly, Chekhov does not mean us to accept at face value Treplyov's harsh verdicts on his mother and her lover. They may truckle to popular demand, but they are not crippled by self-doubt. Arkadina, barnstorming the countryside in the Russian equivalent of *East Lynne*, is convinced that she is performing a public service; her stage name ambivalently refers both to Arcadia and to a garish amusement park in St. Petersburg. Trigorin, well aware that he is falling short of his masters Tolstoy and Turgenev, still plugs away in the tradition of well-observed realism.

Treplyov and Trigorin cannot be set up as hostile antitheses, for, as the Soviet critic Chudakov has said, they 'themselves call their basic theses into question'.[6] Treplyov's desire for new forms is a more vociferous and less knowing version of Trigorin's self-deprecation. The younger writer scorns the elder as a *belletrist*, but by the play's end, he is longing to find similar formulas by which to avoid journalese. Arkadina may not have read her son's work ('No time') and Trigorin may not have cut the pages on any story but his own; but Treplyov himself admits he has never read Trigorin's stuff, thus partaking of their casual egoism. A more productive antithesis than that of Treplyov-Trigorin, who both contain elements of Chekhov himself, might be a polarity of idealism and art, with Treplyov at one end, and the schoolmaster Medvedenko, all purblind financial worries, at the other. The two men are linked by Masha, who loves the young writer ('He has . . . the look of a poet') and is loved by the teacher. Each act opens with her statement of the hopelessness of her situation, moving from the affected pose of 'I am in mourning for my life' to the flat acceptance of 'unrequited love – that's only for novels'. She and Nina are to be contrasted in the uneasy terms with which they deal with their frustrated hopes.

The literary critic Prince Mirsky pointed out that *bezdarnost* ('giftlessness' or 'lack of talent') was a 'characteristically Chekhovian word'[7]; for it sums up an absence of positive qualities. Chekhov once defined talent as the ability 'to distinguish important evidence from unimportant' (to Suvorin, 30 May 1888). In *The Seagull*, the word 'talent' is the touchstone by which the characters evaluate themselves and one another. Treplyov begins by feeling he is a nobody among the actors and writers that crowd his mother's salon: he claims to have 'no talent at all'. But he rebukes Nina for considering him 'a mediocrity, a nonentity' and points scornfully at Trigorin as a 'genuine talent'. In her anger, Arkadina lashes out at her son by referring to 'people with no talent and lots of pretensions', and when he retaliates 'I've got more talent than the lot of you put together,' she crushes him by uttering his own thought: 'You nobody'. In Act One, Arkadina encourages Nina to go on the stage by saying 'You must have talent'; in the last act, Treplyov grudgingly states 'she showed some talent at screaming or dying'. Trigorin complains that his public regards him as no more than 'charming and talented,' yet when Arkadina caresses him with 'You're so talented,' he succumbs to her blandishments.

The point is that 'talent' exists independently of human relations and can be consummated in isolation. To be talented is not necessarily to be a superior person. As usual, Dorn sees most acutely to the heart of the matter: 'you're a talented fellow,' he tells Treplyov, but 'without a well-defined goal . . . your talent will destroy you'. Tactlessly in

Arkadina's presence, he had declared 'there aren't many brilliant talents around these days . . . but the average actor has improved greatly'. Sharing Chekhov's distrust of the grand gesture, Dorn prefers the amelioration of the general lot to artistic supermen. Nina, who had idealised Arkadina and Trigorin as 'a celebrated actress' and 'a famous author' to whom commoners must defer, finally recognises that fame and glamour are less important than staying power.

Treplyov's one display of talent, his symbolist play located in a void where all things are extinct and the only conflicts are between the Universal Will and the Principle of Eternal Matter, may seem like parody. But Chekhov is careful to place the harsh criticism on the lips of Arkadina, whose taste and motives are suspect, and Nina, who complains that it is nothing but *chitka*, literally a 'reading,' a technical term she may have picked up from Arkadina. Chekhov is not ridiculing Treplyov for his espousal of new forms, something he himself had predicted might take a hundred years to evolve. Treplyov's shortcoming is his inability to preserve the purity of his ideal; his symbolist venture is actually a garble of popular stage techniques ill-connected to his poetic aspirations. The devil's red eyes are, as Arkadina observes, 'special effects'. His theatre, 'Curtain, first grooves, second grooves, and beyond that, empty space' is an amateur mock-up of Lentovsky's Fantasy Theatre in Moscow, relying on the gloom and the damp for atmosphere. He seems unable to find an original way of expressing his nebulous ideas; his play, like Bjørnson's *Beyond Human Power*, 'has no significance because the idea isn't clear. It's impossible to make one's characters perform miracles, when you yourself have no sharply defined conviction as to miracles' (to Suvorin, 20 June 1896). In his notebooks, Chekhov stressed, 'Treplyov has no fixed goals and that's what destroyed him. Talent destroyed him'.

Chekhov, however, did manage in *The Seagull* to initiate his own new form, incomplete and transitional though it may be. For the first time, he did away with 'French scenes,' allowing each act to develop not through the artificial entrances and exits of characters, but by a concealed inner dynamic. The overall rhythm of the play is also carefully scored. 'I wrote it forte and ended it pianissimo, contrary to all the rules of dramatic art' (to Suvorin, 21 Nov. 1895). The forte passages occur in the first three acts, which are compressed to within a week's time; there is then the lapse of two years before the pianissimo of Act Four. The characters must fill in the gaps in their and our knowledge by the awkward device of asking one another what's been going on. But this apparently clumsy structure derives from Chekhov's anxiety to keep offstage what a traditional playwright would have saved for his obligatory scenes. The most intense and sensational actions – Nina's seduction and abandonment, the death of her child, Trigorin's return to Arkadina, – are, like Treplyov's two suicide attempts, left to our imagination. We are allowed to see the antecedents and consequences, as it were the foreplay and post-coital subsidence, but not the act itself.

The submergence of hyper-dramatic moments, the key to Chekhov's dramatic method, can be noticed halfway through Act One, after Treplyov has rung down the curtain on his play and stormed off. Eventually, Nina emerges from behind the stage, and Arkadina introduces her to Trigorin.

NINA: Oh, I'm so pleased . . . (*Embarrassed.*) I read all your things.
ARKADINA (*seating Nina beside her*). Don't be bashful,

darling. He's a celebrity, but he doesn't put on airs. You see, he's bashful himself.

DORN: I presume we can raise the curtain now, it's spooky like this.

SHAMRAYEV (*loudly*). Yakov, haul up that curtain, boy! (*The curtain is raised.*)

NINA (*to Trigorin*). It's a strange play, isn't it?

TRIGORIN: I didn't understand a word. Nevertheless, I did enjoy watching it. Your acting was so sincere. And the scenery was gorgeous. (*Pause.*) I suppose there are lots of fish in that lake.

NINA: Yes.

TRIGORIN: I love fishing. For me there's no greater pleasure than sitting on the bank at sunset and watching the cork bob up and down.

NINA: But I should think that if someone had pleasure in creating a work of art, he couldn't take pleasure in anything else.

ARKADINA (*laughing*). Don't talk that way. Whenever anyone compliments him, he makes himself scarce.

At which point, Shamrayev launches into his anecdote about the basso Silva, a pause ensues, and Dorn makes his famous remark, 'A silent angel flew by'.

The apparently banal passage is in fact a turning-point for Nina and Trigorin. Their introduction reveals in a few deft strokes the incompatibility of their views of art: Trigorin can proffer only a few platitudes about the play, before turning to a more engaging subject, fishing. (These are, incidentally, two of his mere three speeches in this act, a sign of his displacement in the wild Treplyovian surroundings.) Nina can only express her second-hand notions of artistic creativity. Arkadina plays stage manager, seating Nina, answering for Trigorin and patronizing them both.

But the brilliant *coup de théâtre* is to have the stage curtain taken up during the social ceremony; what might have been merely a naturalistic byblow becomes a symbolic revelation that Treplyov's effort is indeed spent, and the drama of Nina and Trigorin is about to begin. The pause that follows Shamrayev's story marks a first intermission, during which the liaison between the two is tacitly forged.

The two-year hiatus between the third and fourth acts stresses the recurrent theme of memory. The past is always idyllic: Arkadina's retrospection of life along the lakeshore, Polina's evocation of her past fling with the Doctor, Shamrayev's anecdotes of antediluvian actors, Sorin's rosy picture of an urban existence are the older generation's forecast of the clashing recollections of Treplyov and Nina. With wry irony, Chekhov divulges each of his characters' insensitivity or obliviousness. 'It's too late,' insists Dr. Dorn when Polina tries to rekindle their earlier affair. 'I don't remember,' shrugs Arkadina when her son recalls her charitable behaviour to an injured laundress. 'I don't remember,' says Trigorin when he is shown the gull he ordered stuffed and mounted in memory of his interview with Nina.

In the last act, the two-year hiatus also sets the characters' development in sharper highlight. Arkadina, Trigorin and the older generation have remained the same; Sorin's stasis has even been intensified by his illness. The only characters to have undergone change are the four young people. Nina and Masha have both compromised their fantasies, Masha by hanging about Treplyov even though she knows her love is hopeless, and Nina by persevering, though aware that stardom is out of her reach. Medvedenko has become more subdued, less anxious to correct his wife; his insistent material worries have modulated into low-keyed domestic fretting. Treplyov has forgotten why he wants to write, although he persists at it. If Nina and Masha are about to turn into pallid versions of Arkadina and Polina, Medvedenko and Treplyov do not have the stamina to become even Shamrayev and Trigorin. The repetition of the monologue from Treplyov's play makes clear the distance travelled between Acts One and Four.

Another new form that Chekhov practised in *The Seagull* was an emblematic progression of locales. The first act is set in 'a portion of the park on Sorin's estate,' where the path to the lake is blocked off by Treplyov's platform stage. This particular region is remote from the main house, and Treplyov has chosen it as his private turf: the characters who come to make up his audience must enter his world of shadows and damp (Polina fears the Doctor will catch cold), and they spend only a brief time there, before returning to safe norms evoked by the strains of the piano drifting into the clearing. Treplyov wants his work of art to be seen as co-existent with nature, with the 'spellbinding lake,' as Dorn calls it; ironically, his man-made stage prevents people from walking to the lake which his mother identifies with 'laughter, noise, shooting, and one romance after another,' ordinary diversions Treplyov disdains. The most casual response to the lake comes from Trigorin who sees it simply as a place to fish.

Act Two moves to Arkadina's territory, a house with a large veranda. The lake can be seen now in the bright light of the sun, not the pallid rays of the moon; but the surrounding verdure is a 'croquet lawn'. Such lawns must be well-kempt, not unlike Arkadina herself, who 'keeps myself in trim, as the saying goes, and I'm always dressed and have my hair done in the latest style'. Notably, Treplyov is the only member of the family circle who does not go into the house during the act. It stands for

Arkadina's hold on life, and from its depths comes the call that keeps Trigorin on the estate.

The dining-room of Act Three brings us into the house; but it is a neutral space, used for solitary meals, changing the dressing on wounds, saying farewells. The act is organized as a series of *tête-à-têtes* which are all the more intense for taking place in a locale no one can call his own. The last act is a drawing-room which Treplyov has turned into a workroom; as the act opens, preparations are being made to convert it to a sickroom. The huddling together of the dying Sorin and the creatively moribund Treplyov implies that they are both 'l'homme qui a voulu' but who never got what he wanted: a wife and a literary career. Once again, Treplyov has tried to establish a space of his own, only to find it overrun by a bustling form of life that ejects him totally by the end. To have a moment alone with Nina, he must close the door to the dining-room and bar it with a chair; when he removes the impediment, the intruders establish a gameroom, and his private act of suicide must happen somewhere else, prefaced by the pathetic fear that 'Mama might be distressed'.

This final locale has a Maeterlinckian tinge, for there is a glass door, used only to admit Nina, who enters romantically enswathed in a *talma*, an enveloping cloak, named after Napoleon's favourite actor. After days spent wandering around the lake, she employs an aperture no other character does, to come in from 'the garden' where 'it's dark ... that stage ... stands bare and unsightly, like a skeleton, and the scene curtain flaps in the wind'. Maeterlinck's dramas are full of mysterious windows and doors that act as entries into another world, beyond which invisible forces are to be intuited and uncanny figures glimpsed. Quoting Turgenev, Nina identifies herself as a homeless wanderer, seeking a haven.[8] But what is 'warm and cosy' to her is claustrophobic and stifling to Treplyov.

In fact, the whole estate acts as a cynosure for the characters' frustrations. Although it has been in Sorin's family for at least two generations – Arkadina recalls playing lotto there as a child, – it is no Turgenevian nest of gentry. None of the characters actually belongs there or feels at home: Arkadina would rather be in an hotel room learning lines; she loses her temper when her wish to go to town is thwarted. Sorin would like to be in an office, hearing street traffic and feels 'as stale as an old cigarette holder'; he sees his nephew going the same way and tries to pry loose some money for a trip abroad. Nina's are always flying visits, time snatched from her oppressed life elsewhere. Medvedenko is there on sufferance. Shamrayev the overseer is a retired military man with no skill as an agricultural manager. Only Trigorin is loath to depart, because, for him, the estate provides enforced idleness. The lake's enchantment can be felt as the spell of Sleeping Beauty's castle: everyone who sets foot there is suspended in time, frozen in place. Real life seems to go on somewhere else.

This symbolic use of environment is better integrated than the more obvious symbol of the seagull. In Ibsen's *The Wild Duck*, the title is of essential importance; all the leading characters are defined by their attitude to the bird, and it exists, unseen, only as they recreate it in their imaginations. The seagull, however, signifies only to three characters: Treplyov who defines it as a symbol, Trigorin who reshapes its symbolic meaning, and Nina who adopts and eventually rejects the symbolism. For Treplyov, it is a means of turning life into art: feeling despised and rejected he shoots the bird as a surrogate martyr, and when the surrogate is in turn rejected, tries to shoot himself. Nina, in Act One, had felt 'lured to the lake like a gull,' but repudiates Treplyov's use of bird imagery for his self-identification. However, when her idol Trigorin spins his yarn about a girl who lives beside a lake, happy and free as a gull, she avidly adopts the *persona*, even though his notion of her freedom is wholly inaccurate. The story turns out to be false, for the man who ruined the bird is not the one who ruins the girl. Nor is Nina ruined in any real sense. She starts to sign her letters to Treplyov 'The Seagull,' which he associates with the mad miller in Pushkin's dramatic poem, 'The Rusalka'. The miller's daughter had been 'ruined' by a prince and drowned herself, leaving her father to run mad and think himself a crow. Both Treplyov and Trigorin thus endeavour to recast Nina as a character in fiction. But when, in the last act, she rejects the sobriquet – 'I'm a seagull. No, not so,' – she is spurning both Treplyov's martyr-bird and Trigorin's novelettish heroine. She survives, if only in an anti-romantic, workaday world.

The varying interpretations to which the seagull is subjected indicate the solipsism in which each character's dream clashes with the others'. A significant speech in the last act has been overlooked because, typically, it seems to be an irrelevance. Dr. Dorn is asked which city he most enjoyed in Europe and he replies 'Genoa,' on account of

The marvellous crowds in the street there. When evening comes and you leave your hotel, the whole street is teeming with people. Then you drift aimlessly into the crowd zigzagging this way and that, you live with its rhythm, you merge with it psychically and you begin to believe that in fact there may be a universal soul, much like the one that Nina Zarechnaya acted in your play once.

Dorn's description presages W. B. Yeats' 1932 poem

1. Georges Wilson and Jean Vilar as Platonov in *Ce Fou de Platonov* at the Théâtre National Populaire, Paris, 1956.

2. Meyerhold's production of *The Proposal* in *33 Swoons*, Moscow, 1935. Igor Ilyinsky as Lomov and Logina as Natasha.

3. Michael Chekhov, the dramatist's nephew, in *A Tragedian in Spite of Himself*, Majestic Theatre, New York, 1935.

4. Simov's setting for acts One and Two of *The Seagull* at the Moscow Art Theatre, 1898.

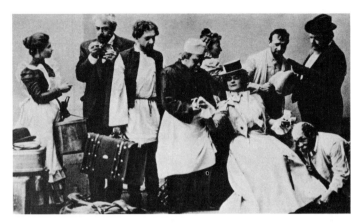

5. *The Seagull* at the Moscow Art Theatre, 1898. End of Act Three:
Stanislavsky as Trigorin (second from left), Olga Knipper as Arkadina
(seated), Vishnevsky as Dorn (far right), Artyom as Shamraev (kneeling).

6. Stephen Haggard as Treplyov and Peggy Ashcroft as Nina in
Komisarjevsky's production of *The Seagull*, New Theatre, London, 1936.

7. Josef Svoboda's design for *The Seagull*, directed by Otomar Krejca at the Narodni Divadlo, Prague, 1960.

8. Retsuke Sugamote as Nina in the first act of *The Seagull*, directed by Andrei Serban for the Shiki Theatre Company, Tokyo, 1980.

9. The final curtain of *Uncle Vanya* at the Moscow Art Theatre, 1900. Mariya Lilina as Sonya (left) and Vishnevsky as Vanya.

10. Sybil Thorndike as Marina and Laurence Olivier as Astrov in *Uncle Vanya* at the National Theatre, London, 1962.

11. Michel St-Denis' *Three Sisters* at the Queen's Theatre, London. From left to right: Frederick Lloyd (Chebutykin), Michael Redgrave (Tusenbach), Peggy Ashcroft (Irina), John Gielgud (Vershinin), Leon Quartermaine (Kulygin).

12. Design for the *Three Sisters* at the Gorki Art Theatre, Moscow, 1940.

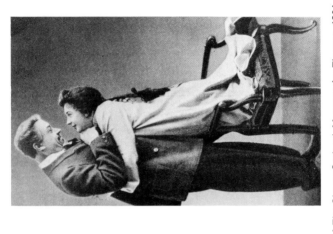

13. Ivan Moskvin as Yepikhodov in the original production of *The Cherry Orchard*, Moscow Art Theatre, 1904.

14. Stanislavsky as Gaev and Lilina as Anya in *The Cherry Orchard*, Moscow Art Theatre, 1904.

'Vacillation,' in which the poet, a 'solitary man' of fifty, sits in a crowded teashop:

> While on the shop and street I gazed
> My body of a sudden blazed;
> And twenty minutes, more or less
> It seemed, so great my happiness,
> That I was blessed and could bless.[9]

This momentary euphoric wholeness is what Dorn experiences by fusion with mankind, and what he and the rest of the characters ordinarily lack. Each one pursues his own appetites and desires; characteristically, Dorn, who chooses to remain aloof from Polina's entreaties, Masha's cries for help, and Sorin's testy dissatisfaction, is also the only one to appreciate Treplyov's play and to be struck by the concept of a Universal Soul. In his recollection of merging with the crowd, he provides a vision, however fleeting, of another kind of life. It was precisely this communal coming-together that the 'mystical anarchists' and other 'decadent' groups were to prescribe as a new form for the theatre of the future.

And yet Chekhov himself does not succumb to this attractive yet passive alternative. Dorn moves into the crowd 'aimlessly,' after having warned Treplyov of the perils of aimlessness. The antagonist in Trigorin's short story ruins a girl because 'he has nothing better to do'. Arkadina ridicules 'this darling country boredom! Hot, quiet, nobody does a thing, everybody philosophises'. Ultimately, Chekhov prefers the active responsibilities contingent on accepting one's lot, even if this means a fate like Nina's.

6
'Uncle Vanya'

The most unendurable thing, to be sure, the really terrible thing,
would be a life without habits, a life which continually required
improvisation. *Nietzsche,* **Die froehliche Wissenschaft** *(1882)*

The premise of *Uncle Vanya* is straightforward. A celebrated Professor of Fine Arts in the capital, now retired on
a reduced income, and married to a young and beautiful
second wife, decides to live on an estate left by his deceased
first wife. Over the years the estate has been managed by
his brother-in-law Ivan Voynitsky and his daughter Sonya,
who sacrificed themselves in the belief that the Professor's
career was luminous and deserving of support. The couple
from Petersburg totally disrupts the even tenor of country
life. Confronted with the Professor's selfish vacuity, Voynitsky regards his own life as wasted and tries to seduce the
languid Yelena. She finds him ridiculous but is in turn
attracted to the cynical and overworked rural doctor
Astrov. Claiming to promote Sonya's interest in him, she
manages both to blight her stepdaughter's hopes and

arouse the doctor's amorous inclinations. The mounting tension culminates in an explosion, when the Professor announces his intention to sell the 'state and move to Finland on the proceeds, thereby stranding his relatives. Desperate, Voynitsky tries to shoot him, fails, and then botches a half-hearted attempt at suicide. Finally, the Professor and Yelena depart, followed by Astrov, leaving the original inhabitants of the estate more isolated, despondent and bereft of illusions than they had been at the start.

Many of Chekhov's contemporaries considered *Uncle Vanya* to be simply *The Wood Demon* revised. For that reason, the Society for Russian Dramatic Authors denied it the Griboedov Prize in 1901. Prince Urusov wrote Chekhov that he had spoiled the earlier play by suppressing Fyodor Orlovsky, omitting Voynitsky's suicide and leaving out the picturesque scene at the mill in Act Four. 'When I related to the French the contents of *The Wood Demon* they were struck just by this: the hero is killed, and life goes on.'[1] But Chekhov had achieved that novelty by the final curtain of *The Seagull*; *Uncle Vanya* moves forward by eschewing even the excitement of a bullet that finds its mark.

Scholars assume that Chekhov finished the play sometime in late 1896, after he had written *The Seagull* but before that comedy had suffered the hapless opening that turned him off playwriting for years. When, in 1897, Nemirovich-Danchenko requested *Uncle Vanya* for the Art Theatre, fresh from its success with *The Seagull*, Chekhov had to explain that he had already promised it to the Maly Theatre. But the dramaturgical committee there, whose members included several professors, was offended by the slurs on Serebryakov's academic career and what it saw as a lack of motivation, and demanded revisions.

Chekhov coolly withdrew *Uncle Vanya* and turned it over to the Moscow Art Theatre, which opened it on 26 October 1899.

Olga Knipper played Yelena and Vishnevsky played Vanya; Stanislavsky, who would have preferred the title role, took to Astrov only gradually. He tended to play his scenes with Yelena as perfervid love interludes, until Chekhov indicated that Astrov's infatuation is easily whistled away. The opening night audience was less than enthusiastic, but the play gained in favour during its run, and soon became a favourite. Gorky wrote to Chekhov: 'I do not consider it a pearl, but I see in it a greater subject than others do; its subject is enormous, symbolistic, and in its form it's something entirely original, something incomparable'.[2]

A useful way of approaching *Uncle Vanya*, and indeed all of Chekhov's late plays, is that suggested by the poet Osip Mandelshtam in an unfinished article of 1936: starting with the cast list.

> What an inexpressive and colorless rebus. Why are they all together? How is the privy counselor related to anybody? Try and define the kinship or connection between Voynitsky, the son of a privy counselor's widow, the mother of the professor's first wife and Sofiya, the professor's young daughter by his first marriage. In order to establish that somebody happens to be somebody else's uncle, one must study the whole roster . . .
>
> A biologist would call this Chekhovian principle ecological. Combination is the decisive factor in Chekhov. There is no action in his drama, there is only propinquity with its resultant unpleasantness.[3]

What Mandelshtam calls 'propinquity' is more important

than the causal connections usually demanded by dramatic necessity, and distinct from naturalistic 'environment'. Chekhov brings his people together on special occasions to watch the collisions and evasions. Conjugal or blood ties prove to be less a determinant on the characters' behaviour than the counter-irritants of their proximity to one another. They are never seen at work in their natural habitats: Arkadina was not on stage or Trigorin in his study, the officers in *Three Sisters* are not in camp, here the Professor has been exiled from his lecture-hall.

The principle is particularly obvious in *Uncle Vanya*, where Chekhov stripped his cast down to the smallest number of any of his full-length plays. He achieved this primarily by conflating the characters of *The Wood Demon*. Khrushchyov's priggishness was diluted by Fyodor's dissipation to form the idealistic but hard-drinking Astrov; Voynitsky's glumness was crossed with Zheltukhin's fussy wooing to compose Vanya. Sofiya the bluestocking and Yuliya the compulsive housekeeper were merged in Sonya. Yelena became less altruistic; and, most significantly, the role of Marina the nanny was added, to provide another, more objective viewpoint.

By reducing the cast to eight (if we exclude the workman), Chekhov could present doublets of each character, to illustrate contrasting reactions to circumstance. Take the Serebryakov/Waffles dyad: the Professor, fond of his academic honours and perquisites, is an old man married to a young woman too repressed to betray him, yet he jealously tyrannises over her. Waffles, whose wife abandoned him almost immediately after their wedding, responded with loving generosity; his life, devoid of honours, is devoted to others. He feels strongly the opprobrium of being 'a sponger', while the Professor is oblivious to his own parasitic position.

Similarly, of the old women, Marina is of the earth earthy, stationary in her obedience to the natural cycle, her life narrowly focussed on barnyard and kitchen; still, she is capable of shrewd comment on human behaviour. Mariya Vasilievna is equally static and narrow, but her eyes never rise from the pages of a pamphlet; she is totally blind to what goes on inside her fellow men. Her reading and Marina's knitting are both palliatives. One, meant for the betterment of all mankind, is sterile; the other, meant for the comfort of specific individuals, is not.

The contrasts are more complex but just as vivid in the younger characters. Sonya and Yelena are both unhappy young women on the threshold of wasted lives; both are tentative and withdrawn in matters of the heart. Sonya, however, is straightforward, less willing to indulge her daydreams, more eager to drug herself with work. Yelena manages to be both indolent and clumsily manipulative in her dealings with others; she declares her affinity to Vanya because they are both 'exasperating' people.

Astrov and Vanya are the only two 'educated persons in the district', who started, like Platonov and Ivanov, with exceptional promise, but grew disillusioned. Astrov's disillusionment was gradual, over years of drudgery as a rural doctor; he has turned into a toper and a cynic, but can still compartmentalise the vestiges of his idealism in his reforestation projects. Vanya's disillusionment came as a thunderclap with the Professor's arrival; its suddenness negated any possibility of maintaining an ideal. Instead, he is diverted to absurd fantasies of bedding down Yelena and, even at a moment of crisis, of thinking himself a potential Dostoevsky or Schopenhauer. His impossible dreams are regularly deflated by Astrov's sarcasm, but both men are, to use a word repeated throughout the play, 'crackpots' ('*chudaki*').

Thus, the propinquity of the characters brings out their salient features; the existence of each puts the other in relief. As in *The Seagull*, they have been collected by Chekhov on an estate where they are displaced persons. We are told it has been in the family for little more than a generation. Vanya relinquished his patrimony to provide his sister's dowry, gave up his own career to cut expenses and work the estate on the Professor's behalf, taking his mother with him: they are acclimatised without being naturalised. The Professor and Yelena are obvious intruders, who disrupt the estate's settled rhythms and cannot accommodate themselves to it. Even Astrov seldom pays a call; he prefers his forests. Only Sonya, Marina and Waffles are rooted in the estate's soil.

Again, the physical progression of the stage setting emblematises the inner development of the action. The play begins outside the house, with a tea-table elaborately set to greet the Professor, who, on his entrance, walks right past it to closet himself in his study. The eruption of appurtenances of gentility into a natural setting vividly suggests the upheaval caused by the Petersburgers' presence. Moreover, the samovar has gone cold during the long wait; it fails to serve its purpose. As is usual with Chekhov the play begins with a couple of characters on stage, waiting for the others to precipitate an event. But when it comes, the event – the tea-party – is frustrated.

The second act moves indoors, its sense of claustrophobia enhanced by the impending storm and Yelena's need to throw open the window. The dining-room too has been usurped by the Professor, who has turned it into a study *cum* sickroom, his medicine littering the sideboard. No family gathers to share a meal: midnight snacks, a clandestine glass of wine, *tête-à-têtes* rather than group encounters are standard. Nanny, who has already grumbled at the altered meal-times, complains that the samovar has still not been cleared. Later she will rejoice that plain noodles have returned in place of the Professor's spicy curries.

In Act Three, the Professor thrusts the family into unfamiliar surroundings when he convenes them in a rarely used reception room. (In the Art Theatre production, the furniture was swathed in dust-covers and the chandelier hung in its bag like a huge teardrop.) Cold, formal, empty, it suits the Professor's taste for his missing podium and further disorients the others. Nanny, cowed by the ambience, must be asked to sit down; for the sake of the occasion, she was prepared to stand at the door like a good servant. Anyone can wander through, like Vanya who intrudes upon Astrov and Yelena with his bunch of roses, another property rendered useless by circumstance.

Finally, in Act Four, we move, for the first time, to a room actually lived in, Vanya's combination bedchamber and estate office. The real life of the house has migrated to this small, cluttered area where day-to-day tasks are carried out, where Astrov has his drawing-table, Sonya her ledgers. There is even a mat for peasants to wipe their feet on. Vanya, like Treplyov, has no personal space that is not encroached on, and none of the objects bespeaks a private being. Once the Professor and Yelena, the disruptive factor, have gone, the family comes together in this atmosphere of warmth generated by routine. But for them to do so, Vanya must abandon his personal claims and ambitions; for good reason a caged linnet chirps by the worktable. The absence of conversation is noticeable in this symbiosis. Were it not for Vanya's impassioned outburst and Sonya's attempts to console him, the characters would write, knit, yawn, read and strum the guitar voicelessly, with no need to communicate aloud, bound together by propinquity.

The more deeply inward the play moves physically, the more the sense of oppression mounts. Chekhov uses weather and seasons along with certain verbal echoes to produce this feeling. In the first few lines of dialogue, Astrov declares, 'It's stifling' (*dushno*), and variations on that sentiment occur with regularity. Vanya repeats it and speaks of Yelena's attempt to muffle her youth; the Professor begins Act Two by announcing that he cannot breathe, and Vanya speaks of being choked by the idea that his life is wasted. Astrov admits he would be suffocated if he had to live in the house for a month. The two young women fling open windows to be able to breathe freely. During the first two acts, a storm is brewing and then rages; and Vanya spends the last act moaning, *Tyazhelo menya*, literally, 'It is heavy to me,' or 'I feel weighed down'. At the very end, Sonya's 'We shall rest' (*My otdokhnyom*) is etymologically related to *dushno* and connotes 'breathing easily'.

Cognate is Yelena's repeated assertion that she is 'shy', in Russian *zastenchivaya*, a word that suggests 'hemmed in, walled up', and might, in context, be better translated 'inhibited'. The references to the Professor's gout, to clouded vision, blood-poisoning and morphine contribute to the numbing atmosphere. This is intensified by the sense of isolation: constant reference is made to the great distances between places. Only Lopakhin the businessman in *The Cherry Orchard* is as insistent as Astrov on how many miles it takes to get somewhere. The cumulative effect is one of immobility and stagnation, oppression and frustration.

Time also acts as a pressure. 'What time is it?' or a statement of the hour is voiced at regular intervals, along with mention of years, seasons, mealtimes. The play begins with Astrov's asking Marina, 'How long is it since we've known each other?', simple exposition but also an initiation of the motif of lives eroded by the steady passage of time. (Chekhov was to reuse this device to launch *Three Sisters* and *The Cherry Orchard.*) *Uncle Vanya* opens at summer's end, proceeds through a wet and dismal autumn, and concludes with a bleak winter staring the characters in the face. The suggestion of summer's evanescence, the equation of middle age with the oncoming fall may seem hackneyed. Vanya certainly leaps for the obvious, with his bouquet of 'mournful autumn roses' and his personalisation of the storm as the pathetic fallacy of his own despair. Chekhov, however, used storms in his short stories as a favourite premonition of a character's mental turmoil, and in stage terms, the storm without and the storm within Vanya's brain effectively collaborate.

The play ends with Sonya's vision of 'a long, long series of days, no end of evenings' to be lived through before the happy release of death. The sense of moments ticking away inexorably is much stronger here than in Chekhov's other plays, because there are no parties, balls, theatricals or fires to break the monotony. The Professor and Yelena have destroyed routine, replacing it with a more troubling sense of torpid leisure. Without the narcotic effect of their daily labour, Astrov, Vanya and Sonya toy with erotic fantasies that make their present all the grimmer.

Beyond these apparent devices, Chekhov is presenting a temporal sequence that is only a segment of the entire conspectus of duration. Another bond with the symbolists is that time in Chekhov's plays resembles Henri Bergson's *temps-fleuve*: human beings can measure duration, but they cannot stand outside the flow. The action of *Uncle Vanya* really began when Vanya gave up his inheritance for his sister's dowry years before; the consequences of that action fill Acts One through Four; but the further consequences remain unknown. How will the Professor and Yelena rub along in the provincial university town of Kharkov (in Chekhov, a symbol of nowhere: in *The Seagull* it adored Arkadina's acting, and in *The Cherry Orchard*, it will be one of Lopakhin's destinations)? How will Astrov manage to avoid alcoholism without the balm of Vanya's conversation and Sonya's solicitude? How will Vanya and Sonya salve their emotional wounds over the course of a lifetime? These questions are left to our imagination.

Samuel Beckett, discussing the blissful pain-killer, habit, referred to 'the perilous zones in the life of an individual, dangerous, precarious, painful, mysterious and fertile, when for a moment the boredom of living is replaced by the suffering of being'.[4] Throughout *Uncle Vanya* the characters, divorced from habit, suffer painful confrontations with being, and by the final curtain, must try hard to return to the dreary but safe addiction to living.

The play's close-knit structure, with its deliberate lack of breadth and breath, is abetted by the thirty-six-hour time scheme, the space limited to the precincts of the house, and the small cast: a tautness not unlike that of neoclassic tragedy. When frustrated passion is compressed so densely, the result approximates Racine. There are confidants (with Yelena as disastrous an adviser to Sonya as Oenone was to Phèdre); interlocking triangles (Vanya loves Yelena who is taken with Astrov who prefers her but is loved by Sonya); tirades (Vanya's night thoughts, Yelena's self-analysis, Astrov's chalk-talk); and a tension between love and duty among the four central characters. This can be heard in Vanya's complaint, 'To betray an old husband you can't stand, that's immoral; to try and muffle the poor youth and living feeling in oneself – that's not immoral.' His contempt for Yelena's code is deprecated by Waffles, himself a cuckold: 'Anyone who betrays a wife or husband is a, I mean, a disloyal person, someone who could even betray his country!'

However, since no passion is ever pushed to its irremediable fulfilment, *Uncle Vanya*, noncommitally subtitled 'Scenes from Country Life',[5] comes closer to comedy. Yelena's name may refer to Helen of Troy, but if so, Chekhov had Offenbach, not Homer, in mind. The play's central irony is that Yelena, who causes so much disruption, is essentially passive. Others regard her as a dynamic force in their lives, but she describes herself (as Calchas had himself) as a 'secondary character', and cannot conceive of making any impact. Feeling trapped, she has no sympathy to waste on other persons' predicaments; even her interest in Sonya is motivated by an attraction to Astrov. Her acceptance of a fleeting kiss and a souvenir pencil as trophies of the romantic upsurge is comically reductive.

The closest approximation to a conventional love scene is that in which Astrov explains his conservation charts to her. In *The Seagull*, Trigorin, in a similar scene, had sought to dispel Nina's rose-tinted fantasies about a writer's life, but the two of them never truly communicated. Trigorin simply expatiated on his own craftsman's obsession, and Nina felt her ideals fortified. In *Uncle Vanya*, the country doctor, galloping apace on his hobbyhorse, gets caught up in his noble dreams for the future, unaware that his audience is preoccupied with personal matters. The professional man is now the idealist, the woman the pragmatist. To Chekhov, Trigorin's self-deprecation had more authenticity than Nina's fantasies; here Astrov's ambitions have more validity than Yelena's intriguing. Eventually, Astrov denigrates his own temptation to philandering by a facetious reference to 'Turgenevian woodland glades'. He signals that tragedy has been averted when he bids Yelena farewell: 'And so, wherever you and your husband set foot, destruction follows in your wake . . . I'm joking, of course, but all the same, it's peculiar, and I'm convinced that if you were to stay, the havoc wreaked would be stupendous'. Instead, *finita la commedia*.

The anti-tragic tendency of the play is apparent in the title. Most serious Russian drama of the 1890s bore titles of symbolic import: *Gold* and *The Price of Life* (Nemirovich-Danchenko), *Chains* (Sumbatov), *At the Bottom* (*The Lower Depths*) (Gorky), *Walls* (Naydyonov). Or a play might be named after its protagonist (Suvorin's *Tatyana Repina*) or a central relationship (Naydyonov's *Vanyushin's Children*). As a rule, Chekhov complies with this convention.

In *Uncle Vanya*, though, the title reveals that the centre of attention is not Astrov, whose attractive qualities can upstage the title role in production, but the self-pitying Voynitsky. Our Uncle Jack, as he might be in English, sounds peripheral, the archetype of mediocrity. Such a man is not serious enough to be given a grownup name; he counts chiefly in relationship to others. But who calls him Uncle Vanya? To the Professor, Yelena and Astrov he is Ivan Petrovich, except when they mean to be slighting. 'That Uncle Vanya' is how Yelena dismisses him in Act Three, and in Act Four Astrov flippantly calls for an embrace before 'Uncle Vanya' comes in. To his mother, he is Jean, the 'radiant personality' of his youth. He is Vanya primarily to Sonya and Waffles, who love him. Therefore, if Voynitsky matters most when he is Uncle Vanya, his self-realisation lies not in competing with the Professor or winning Yelena,[6] but in his dealings with his dependents. He gave up trying to be Jean long ago; when he stops trying to be Ivan Petrovich and fulfills himself as Uncle Vanya, a new life might commence.

Just as Ivan Petrovich is effaced by Uncle Vanya, so the

theme of blighted or unrequited love must play second
fiddle to that of meaningful work. Chekhov's own activities
as a country doctor, farmer, planter of trees, set an example
for his characters, who, in his play, can be divided between
those who perform useful tasks, and those whose occupa-
tions are meaningless. Two crucial transmitters of this
theme are the catchphrase *Nado delo delat* and Sonya's
final 'aria.'

Nado delo delat has been translated as 'We must work,'
which sounds ironic, since it drops from the lips of two such
dilettanti as Vanya's mother and the Professor. But the
phrase is more topical in its connotations: it means 'One
must do something, one must take an active part,' and
alludes to Chernyshevsky's radical novel of 1864, *Chto
delat? (What is to be done?)*. 'Something must be done' is
therefore an out-of-date propaganda slogan, still current
with Mariya Vasilyevna who chews over the liberalism of a
bygone generation (like Roebuck Ramsden in Shaw's *Man
and Superman*) and the Professor who (like Gayev in *The
Cherry Orchard*) is a 'man of the 'eighties', a right-minded
but essentially quiescent intellectual during the repressive
regime of Aleksandr III whose name the Professor bears.
This was picked up by the original audiences, who thought
Chekhov was mocking the liberal movement, for he is not
assailing the characters' laziness so much as their armchair
progressivism and hollow phrasemaking. Talk is cheap.

Sonya and Vanya, at the play's end, seem bereft,
marooned by those on whom they had pinned their hopes.
Vanya cannot bear up under the disappointment and
dissolves into tears, at which point Sonya tries to console
him with her vision of Nirvana and the possible blessing of
posterity. Vanya's plaints have been mingled with the
humdrum recitation of accounts, a device which Chekhov
may have borrowed from Sumbatov's play *Chains* (1887),

a work he admired. In Sumbatov, the consoler is a plain-spoken middle-aged woman, an authority figure; her patient is a nervous young spinster. Chekhov reverses the relationship; the young spinster recommends work for the older authority figure. Sonya acts *in loco parentis* and her counsel of patience has the same soothing but empty effect as Marina's cooling offer of lime-flower tea had on the Professor. Nothingness as a consolation prize is not necessarily endorsed by Chekhov, as it is by Strindberg in his dream plays. Nevertheless, in the words of an American critic, 'The inertia of the spirit in Chekhov is there as a blessing as well as a curse'.[7]

In *Uncle Vanya* Chekhov was transferring to the theatre the ability to pose questions without solving them, to suggest life beyond the last page that had hitherto been the exclusive property of the novel. Ibsen had already pioneered in dramatising the repercussions of private life; his plays reverberate with larger ethical and even cosmic considerations. There the tension in reconciling self-fulfilment with a hostile world has an heroic tinge, even when a Mrs. Alving or a John Gabriel Borkman falls. But, as the director Meyerhold pointed out, in Chekhov, there can be no tragic hero, only 'a group of persons devoid of a center'.[8] The contradictory needs for self-fulfilment can never be consummated so long as they share this discordant 'propinquity'.

7
'Three Sisters'

The father a famous general, nice pictures, expensive furniture;
he died; the daughters had a good education, but are slovenly in
appearance, read little, go horseback riding, are boring.
Chekhov's **Notebook I**, *p. 130.*

At the urging of the Moscow Art Theatre, Chekhov set
about to write them a play. With specific actors in mind for
given roles and, mindful too of the Art Theatre's strengths,
Chekhov spent more time in the composition of *Three
Sisters*, than on any of his earlier dramas. He was especially
anxious to cut out superfluities in monologues and provide
a sense of movement.[1]

At the core of the play stood the three daughters of an
army officer who had spent their earliest youth in Moscow,
but moved to the provinces when their father was trans-
ferred there as Brigadier General. The eldest, Olga, is a
mistress in the local school; the middle sister, Masha,
marries a classics instructor in the same institution; the
youngest, Irina, is just turning eighteen when the play

begins. They have invested a good deal of hope in their brother Andrey, who is supposed to become a professor and bring them back to Moscow, the scene of their happiest memories. But life supervenes. Andrey marries a local *bourgeoise*, Natasha, who proceeds to take over the sisters' home and force them into peripheral positions. Masha tries to lose herself in an affair with an unhappily married man, Colonel Vershinin, whose regiment is temporarily stationed in the town. Irina listlessly entertains two suitors, the insipid Baron Tusenbach and the enigmatic and surly Solyony. Olga unwillingly rises in the academic hierarchy. Ultimately these pastimes lead nowhere. By the play's end, Vershinin departs with his regiment, Solyony kills the Baron in a senseless duel, and Natasha and her children victoriously occupy the house. Against a mocking chorus provided by their former tenant, the nihilistic Army Doctor Chebutykhin, the sisters cling to some last vestiges of hope in order to survive.

Unfortunately, when the Art Theatre actors heard the author read the play for the first time, in October 1900, they were sorely disappointed. 'This is no play, it's only an outline' was the immediate reaction.[2] Chekhov sedulously reworked it all, and in the process added many striking touches. The ironic counterpoint of Tusenbach's and Chebutykin's remarks in Acts One and Four, most of Solyony's pungent lines, Masha's quotation from *Ruslan and Lyudmila* about the curved seastrand were added at this stage. It is wonderful to think that only while revising did Chekhov decide to leave her on stage for the final tableau.

Chekhov sat in on the early rehearsals, and insisted that a colonel be in attendance to instruct the actors in proper military deportment; he personally orchestrated the fire-bell sound effects for Act Three. He put the greatest emphasis on that act, which, he insisted, must be performed quietly and with weariness (to Knipper, 17 and 20 January 1901). When Stanislavsky proposed that Natasha cross the stage at the beginning of the act, looking under furniture for burglars, Chekhov riposted that her silent crossing with a candle 'à la Lady Macbeth' would be more 'horrible'. On the other hand, Stanislavsky requested the suppression of a stage direction that required Tusenbach's corpse to be carried across the upstage area during the play's final speeches: too many extras, too much noise and distraction, and an inevitable wobbling of the backdrop were his grounds. Chekhov complied.

Three Sisters opened at the Art Theatre on 31 January 1901, with Stanislavsky as Vershinin, Olga Knipper as Masha, Meyerhold as Tusenbach and Vishnevsky as Kulygin. Although many critics were put off by the play's seeming hopelessness and what struck them as vague motivation in the characters, the production was acclaimed by the public. 'It's music, not acting', asserted Gorky. The great actress Yermolova, who, years before, had turned down the fledgling dramatist's *Without Patrimony*, declared that at last she realised what the Art Theatre was getting at.

The writer Leonid Andreyev attended the thirtieth performance, despite a friend's warning that its effect would be suicidally depressing. Quite against expectation, he found himself totally drawn into the play by the middle of Act One; no longer appraising the scenery or the actors, he became convinced that 'the story of the three sisters . . . is not an invention, not a fantasy, but a fact, an event, something every bit as real as stock options at the Savings & Loan'. By the end, he, with the rest of the audience, was in tears, but his dominant impression was not pessimistic. For Andreyev, the residual effect, the pervasive mood, the play's basic 'tragic melody' was a yearning for life. 'Like steam, life can be compressed into a narrow little container, but, also like steam, it will endure pressure only to a certain degree. And in *Three Sisters*, this pressure is brought to the limit, beyond which it will explode, – and don't you in fact hear how life is seething, doesn't its angrily protesting voice reach your ears?'[4]

This reaction was due in part to the play's early run coinciding with student riots; consequently the characters' aspirations were identified with topical political sentiment. It was due as well to the theatre's remarkably veristic production and its careful transmission of mood. Eventually, theatregoers would say not that they were going to the Art Theatre to view *Three Sisters*, but that they were 'paying a call on the Prozorovs.' Chekhov's technique, however, provided the premises for this illusion of reality.

The American poet Randall Jarrell has compared Chekhov's method in *Three Sisters* to that of the painter Edouard Vuillard.

> In certain of his indoor and outdoor scenes of French domestic life, the foundation areas on the canvas are made less emphatic by the swarms of particles that mottle the walls with rose-printed paper, the rugs with swirls, the lawns with pools of sun and shade. From such variation and variegation comes his cohesion. Vuillard commingles plaids and dappled things as non sequitur as the jottings in Chebutykin's notebook.[5]

And Jarrell made lists of what he called 'Vuillard spots' in the play: apparently random speech habits, mannerisms, personality traits and incidents that add up to a character or an action.

It is a stimulating analogy, useful in revealing what is new about *Three Sisters*. To extend the metaphor, this is the first time Chekhov employs a broad canvas devoid of exclusively foreground figures – no Ivanovs or Platonovs, not even Treplyovs or Vanyas; the sisters must share their space, in every sense, with Natasha, Tusenbach and Solyony. There are no more soliloquys: almost never is a character left alone on stage. The propinquity factor is very much at work. Andrey must pour out his discontents to deaf Ferapont, and Masha must announce her adulterous love to the stopped-up ears of her sister Olga. *Têtes-à-têtes* are of the briefest: no more Trigorin spinning out a description of his career or Astrov explicating maps to prospective paramours. Vershinin and Tusenbach spout their speeches about work and the future to a room full of auditors. Anyone arranging a rehearsal schedule of the play will soon discover that most of the actors must be on call most of the time, to provide the 'Vuillard spots' that compose the whole picture.

Those rhetorical paeans of Vershinin and Tusenbach have been cited as Utopian alternatives to the dreary provincial life depicted on stage. True, the men who formulate them are ineffectual, with no chance of realising their 'thick-coming fancies'. But the monologues do work as a meliorative element. In *Dead Souls*, the comic epic of Nikolay Gogol, Chekhov's favourite writer, lyric digressions and rambling speculations by the narrator are used to supply an idyllic, idealised contrast to the squalid action in the foreground. Chekhov, deprived of the narrative element, must put into the mouths of his characters visions of an improved life. The imagery of birds of passage, birch trees, flowing rivers sounds a note of freshness and harmony that highlights all the more acutely the characters' inability to get in touch with the spontaneous and the natural. The cranes are programmed to fly, 'and whatever thoughts, sublime or trivial, drift through their heads, they'll keep on flying, not knowing why or whither'.

The most blatant call for an alternative is the sisters' recurrent plaint, 'To Moscow, to Moscow!' Almost from the play's première, critics wondered what was stopping the Prozorovs from buying a ticket to the big city. Obviously, Moscow is a Holy Grail, envisaged differently by each character. Andrey sees it not only as a university town, but as the site of great restaurants, while for old Ferapont it marks the locale of a legendary pancake-fest. Vershinin gloomily recalls a grim bridge and roaring water there, Solyony has invented a second university for it, and Olga looks back to a funeral. No clear image of Moscow emerges from the medley of impressions, so that it remains somewhere over the rainbow, just out of sight.

But because the sisters are fixated on this distant point, commentators and directors have constantly inflated them into heroines. Too frequently, the play is reduced to a conflict between three superwomen and a ravening bitch: the sensitive and high-strung Prozorovs can be no match for the ruthless life-force embodied in Natasha, and so they succumb, albeit preserving their ideals. This common interpretation is not borne out by a close examination of a play, which Chekhov said had *four* heroines. As the Rumanian critic Jovan Hristić has shrewdly noted, the three of the title are 'true spiritual sisters of Hedda Gabler, who corrupt everything around them by dint of thinking themselves superior'.[6] The analogy works on several levels, from the military upbringing to the ultimate downfall, engineered partly by an instinctual bourgeoise (Natasha for Thea Elvsted), a second-rate academic (Andrey for Tesman), and an inept idealist (Vershinin for Løvborg). Like Hedda, the three sisters are at variance with their environment, which represents for them common vulgarity;

Masha's scorn of civilians is bitter. The play chronicles the town's encroachment on their lives, as Olga becomes part of the educational system, Irina a cog in the civil bureaucracy, Andrey a fixture on the County Council, and Masha in enforced attendance at faculty parties. By the last act, the stage direction informs us that their backyard has become a kind of empty lot, across which the townsfolk tramp when necessary. It is the next step after the fire, when the townsfolk invaded their home and bore off their old clothes. And, of course, Natasha's infiltrations and that of her lover and town's *de facto* head, the unseen Protopopov, began earliest of all.

To protect themselves against this encroachment, the sisters have erected a paling of culture, and within it, they have invited the military. For once, Chekhov does not use outsiders as a disruptive force; for the sisters, the soldiers spell colour, excitement, life. But the factitiousness of this glamour is soon apparent: a peacetime army is a symbol of idleness and pointless expense. Men trained to fight while away their time philosophising and playing the piano, teaching gymnastics and reading the paper, carrying on backstairs love affairs and fighting duels. The sisters have pinned their hopes on a regiment of straw men. It is hard to determine who is the weaker, Vershinin, forecasting future happiness while unable to break with his psychotic wife, or Tusenbach, whose noble sentiments are belied by his unprepossessing appearance and unassertive manner. Chekhov relentlessly moves through the ranks to show Solyony as a vainglorious bully, Chebutykin as an incompetent doctor, and Fedotik as a toy-loving child. These are carpet knights, suitable for dressing out a party (like the Captain in *The Wedding*), but not for salvaging anyone's life. That the sisters should make such a fuss about them reveals at once the irreality of their values.

Similarly, if culture, in the sense of refined feelings revealed through sensitivity and cultivated understanding, is the touchstone for the Prozorovs, it will not sustain scrutiny either. The term *intelligentsia* is misleadingly translated as 'intellectuals,' when it simply means those persons who had enjoyed a higher education. For Russians, it bore a burden of political awareness, social commitment and an obligation to those benighted souls who did not share the *intelligent*'s advantages. The Prozorov family prides itself on these virtues, and judges others by them. Many of the major characters are closely connected with the school system. Olga is somewhat unwillingly promoted from teacher to headmistress, and despite her complaints and exhaustion, it is that work which enables her to maintain her independence and create a haven for her old nanny. Kulygin is a tutelary careerist, truckling to the principal and turning Masha into a faculty wife. Andrey's father had intended him for a professor in Moscow, and his sisters make him feel guilty for missing this goal. On the scale of failed but honourable *intelligents* that includes Ivanov and Vanya, Andrey, with his gambling and whining, is a despicable come-down.

When tested by the realities of life, the fabric of their culture soon falls to pieces. The Prozorovs and their circle cling to the shreds and patches – Latin tags for Kulygin, quotations from Pushkin, Krylov and Lermontov for Masha and Solyony, amateur music. Andrey's 'sawing away' at the violin and Masha's untested prowess at the keyboard are mocked in the last act by Natasha's offstage rendition of 'The Maiden's Prayer'. Irina grieves that she cannot remember the Italian for window, as if foreign vocabulary could buoy her up in the sea of despair. Solyony poses as the romantic poet Lermontov, but his ultimate behaviour shows him to be more like Martynov, the man who killed Lermontov in a duel. During the fire, Natasha condescendingly must remind Olga of the *intelligent*'s duty 'to help the poor. It's an obligation of the rich'. Philosophising (always a pejorative word for Chekhov) passes for thought, snippets from the newspaper ('Balzac was married in Berdichev') pass for knowledge, a superior attitude passes for delicacy of feeling, yet everyone's conduct dissolves into rudeness or immorality.

At one moment in the Brecht and Weill opera *The Rise and Fall of the City of Mahagonny*, a whore is playing 'The Maiden's Prayer' and a roughhewn client takes the cigar out of his mouth and comments, 'Das ist die ewige Kunst' ('Such is eternal art'). Chekhov's technique is considerably more subtle, but his inferences are not dissimilar. *Three Sisters* does not try to show how three gifted women were defeated by a philistine environment, but rather that their unhappiness is of their own making; if they are subjugated and evicted by the Natashas of this world, it is because they have not recognized and dealt with their own shortcomings. At one point or another, each of the sisters is as callous and purblind as Natasha herself. Olga rather cattily criticises Natasha's belt at the party, though she has been told that the girl is shy in company; in Act Three, she refuses to listen to Masha's avowal of love, will not voluntarily face facts. Her very removal to a garret is as much an avoidance of involvement as it is an exile imposed by Natasha. Irina is remarkably unpleasant to both her suitors, Tusenbach and Solyony; in her post as telegraph clerk she is abrupt to a grieving mother; and at the last refuses to say the few words of love that might solace the Baron, even though, as Chekhov informed Olga Knipper, she is prescient of an impending misfortune. Masha talks like a trooper, drinks, abuses Anfisa almost as badly and with less excuse than Natasha does. Her flagrant adultery with Vershinin may even be more destructive than Natasha's with Protopopov, for Kulygin genuinely loves his wife, whereas Andrey tries to forget that he has one.

This litany of faults is not meant to blacken the sisters or to exonerate Natasha, Solyony and the others. It is meant to redress the balance: Chekhov selects the Prozorov family (who, along with the officers, were based on acquaintances) to sum up a way of life. With all the benefits of education, a loving home and creature comforts, the sisters stagnate, not simply because they live in the sticks, but because they have established nothing of value to give meaning to their existence. The ennobling labour that Tusenbach and Vershinin rhapsodise over, that inspires Irina, cannot be equated with doing a job every day. Olga's teaching, Irina's work at the Council and the telegraph office, the position at the mines to which Tusenbach retires offer a prospect of meaningless drudgery.

The abiding state of mind is to be 'fed up' (*nadoelo*). In his brief moment alone with Masha in Act Two, Vershinin blames the average local *intelligent* for being 'fed up with his wife, fed up with his estate, fed up with his horses'; but he is clearly characterising himself, for he soon draws a picture of his own wretched marriage. Masha, whom Vershinin would exempt as an exceptional person, is 'fed up with winter', and when her husband proclaims his love with 'I'm so content,' she bitterly spits back, 'I'm fed up, fed up, fed up'. Even the genteel Olga pronounces herself 'fed up'·with the fire. The unanimous response to this spiritual sickness unto death is a commonplace fatalism. Chebutykin's 'It's all the same' (*Vsyo ravno*) is echoed by most of the characters. Vershinin quotes it when denying differences between the military and civilians; Tusenbach describes his resignation from the army in those words; Solyony dismisses his love for Irina with the phrase.

According to Irina, Andrey's debts are *vsyo ravno* to Natasha. This willed insouciance is the counterbalance to the equally deliberate velleities about the future.

To represent the slow disintegration of these lives, *Three Sisters* unfolds over a longer period than any of Chekhov's other plays. It begins on the fifth of May, Irina's twentieth nameday, and ends in autumn, four years later. The characters talk incessantly about time, from the very first line, 'Our father died, just a year ago today,' almost to the last. The passage of time is denoted by such obvious tokens as Natasha's growing children, Andrey's problem with overweight, Olga's promotions. However, this is more than a family chronicle. Chekhov insists on the subjectivity of time, what Dr. Johnson called its 'elasticity'. Each act indicates that what had gone before is now irrevocably swallowed up, lost not simply in the distant past, but in what had been yesterday. The youth in Moscow, aglow with promise, to which the sisters retrospect is undercut by their initial response to its survivor, Vershinin: 'Oh, how you've aged!' The party of Act One is spoken of in Act Two, a few months later, as if it belonged to a bygone Golden Age; by Act Three, Tusenbach is referring to it as 'Back in those days'. Time measures the increasing negativity of life: it has been two years since the doctor drank, three years since Masha played the piano, or maybe four. It's been a long time since Andrey played cards, i.e., the few months since Act Two. If time passes in a steady process of diminution, perspectives into the future are not enough to replace the losses. Chebutykin smashes a valuable clock, demolishing time, but his chiming watch in the last act continues to announce fresh departures.

Setting up markers for time, Chekhov structures each act around a special event that catalyses routine responses and sticks in the memory. Irina's nameday party serves a number of dramatic functions: it commemorates a date, assembles all the characters in one place, and is the highwater mark for the sisters' hope. It is the last time we see them as sole mistresses in their own domain; each of them is on the verge of a promising situation. Coming-of-age opens the world to Irina; the arrival of Vershinin enlivens Masha; and Olga still enjoys teaching. The Shrovetide party in Act Two is a sharp contrast: it takes place after dark, with several habitués absent (Olga must work late as must Kulygin, Vershinin is called away by his wife's suicide attempt). Twice the party is broken up by Natasha, and finally the revellers realize that amusement is to be sought outside the home. No tea is forthcoming from the usurper Natasha any more than carriage horses were from the insolent overseer Shamraev in *The Seagull*.

The eating at these events, the metaphor for shared experience, disintegrates as the play proceeds. Act One had ended with the cast gathered round the table, regaling themselves with roast turkey, apple pie and too much vodka. The odd men out were Natasha and Andrey, furtively conducting their romance at a remove from the teasing family. But in Act Two, Natasha is now seated at the festive board, criticising the table manners of others; Solyony has eaten up all the chocolates. The Caucasian mutton dish *chekhartma* becomes a bone of angry contention. Once Natasha gains a foothold, the indiscriminate feeding ends.

The fire in Act Three is a *tour de force*; physical danger, mass hysteria and crowd movement, although kept off-stage, have forced the characters into their present situation, both topographically and emotionally. Gradually, like Andreyev's image of steam rising in a boiler, all of them are pushed upwards into the compressed space under the eaves. Even though the conflagration does not singe the

Prozorov house, it creates this thermodynamic effect. Exhausted or drunken, in some way exacerbated by the calamity, the characters pour out their feelings and then leave. It is the most hysterical of all the acts and the most confessional. To no avail does Olga protest, 'I'm not listening, I'm not listening!' Ibsen in *Ghosts* and Strindberg in his last plays used the image of fire to represent the end of a world of lies, the last judgement that will purify mankind and reveal the truth. In *Three Sisters*, the fire leaves the sisters unpurified, although their world is rapidly being consumed; amid the desolation, they are simply charred.

Once again, Chekhov constrains his characters to come in contact by preventing privacy. One would expect the bedroom of an old-maid schoolteacher and a young virgin to be the most sacrosanct of chambers; but through a concatenation of circumstances it turns into Grand Central Station, from which intruders like Solyony must be forcibly ejected. The space is an intimate one, just right for playing out intimate crises; but the confessions and secrets are made to detonate in public. The Doctor's drunken creed of nihilism, Andrey's exasperation with his wife, Masha's confession of her adultery, even when addressed to unwilling hearers cowering behind a screen, become public events.

Or else the private moment is neutralised by submersion in minutiae. Masha makes up her mind to elope with Vershinin. Traditionally, this would be a major dramatic turning-point, the crux when the heroine undergoes her peripeteia. Here, the decision is lost amid plans for a charity recital, Tusenbach's snoring and other people's personal problems. The chance tryst offered by the fire trivialises Masha's and Vershinin's love because it projects it against a background of civic disaster. Even their love-song has been reduced to 'Ta-ram-tam-tam', the humming of an aria from Tchaikovsky's *Yevgeny Onegin*. In other words, what is crucial to some of the characters is always irrelevant or unknown to the others, much as the seagull had been. It may, ultimately, be no more significant than the hand-me-down garments which are useless to Olga but of prime importance to the fire victims. This impartiality of Chekhov's in meting out consequence is not unlike Alfred Jarry's absurdist 'pataphysical axiom, that truth lies only in exceptions, or, as Chebutykin keeps saying, 'It's all the same'. Chekhov, however, does not insist on the impossibility of values and communication; he simply believes that the attribution of value cannot be made by myopic mortals.

The last act adjusts the angle of vantage. There is very little recollection in it, but a good deal of futile straining towards the future. A brief time has elapsed between Act Three, when the regiment's departure was off-handedly mentioned, and Act Four, when it occurs. The departure is so abrupt an end to the sisters' consoling illusions that they cannot bring themselves to allude to the past. Henceforth they will be thrown back on their resources. The play had begun with them lording it over the drawingroom, but now they are cast into the yard. Olga lives at the school, Masha refuses to go into the house, Andrey wanders about with the pram like a soul in limbo. Food has lost its ability to comfort. The Baron must go off to his death without his morning coffee, while Andrey equates goose and cabbage with the deadly grip of matrimony. Each movement away is accompanied musically: the regiment leaves to the cheery strains of a marching band, the piano tinkles to the lovemaking of Natasha and Protopopov, and the Doctor sings 'Ta-ra-ra-boom-de-ay'. The bereft sisters standing in the yard are made to seem out of tune.

115

The final tableau, with the sisters clinging to one another and intoning, 'If only we knew, if only we knew,' has been played optimistically, as if the dawn of a bright tomorrow did lie just beyond the horizon. But the time to come that Olga evokes has lost the rosy tinge of Vershinin's and Tusenbach's improvisations. Like Sonya's aria in *Uncle Vanya*, it predicts a void, that must be filled. The disillusionment of the four hours' traffic on the stage and the four years' passage of time has aged the sisters, but not enlightened them. They still, in William Blake's words, 'nurse unacted desires,' still are not on speaking terms with their lives. Directors who want an upbeat ending eliminate Doctor Chebutykin from this moment, but Chekhov placed him there to prevent this final descant from being taken at face value. The music-hall chorus he sings had Russian lyrics (which would be known to everyone in the original audience), 'I'm sitting on a curb-stone / Bitterly crying / 'Cause I don't know much'. The implied mockery shows Olga's 'If we only knew, if we only knew' to be an absurd wish. It is a laconic equivalent of the final chorus in *Oedipus the King*: 'Count no man fortunate till he is dead'. Sophocles warned human beings not to assume they know their place in the divine scheme of things. Chekhov's antiphonal chorus of Olga and Chebutykin hymns the impossibility of such awareness, and the need to soldier on, despite that disability.

8
'The Cherry Orchard'

Symbolism is the inadvertent rainbow on the waterfall of reality.
Andrey Bely, 'Theatre & Modern Drama' (1908)

'The next play I write will definitely be funny, very funny, at
least in concept,' Chekhov stated to his wife (7 Mar 1901),
once *Three Sisters* had opened. This concept, as the author
sketched it to Stanislavsky, would incorporate a footman
mad about fishing (a part written for Artyom, the original
Chebutykin), a garrulous, one-armed billiard player (to be
enacted by Vishnevsky), and a situation in which the
landowner is continually borrowing money from the footman. He also envisaged a branch of flowering cherry thrust
through a window of the manor house.

Actually, Chekhov's notebooks reveal that *The Cherry
Orchard* had taken root even earlier, with the governess
Charlotta, another farcical type, and the idea that 'the
estate will soon go under the hammer' the next ramifica-
tion. The theme had a personal application. For the boy
Chekhov, the sale of his home had been desolating. This

117

imminent loss of one's residence looms over *Without Patrimony*, becomes the (literal) trigger of *Uncle Vanya*, and gives an underlying dynamic to *Three Sisters*.

The endangered estate, in Chekhov's early plans, was to belong to a liberal-minded old lady who dressed like a girl (shades of Arkadina), smoked and couldn't do without society, a sympathetic sort tailored to the Maly Theatre's Olga Sadovskaya, who specialised in Ostrovskyan hags. When the Maly Theatre refused to release her, Chekhov rejuvenated the role until it was suitable for someone of Olga Knipper's age. Only then did he conceive of Lopakhin. Varya first appeared as a grotesquely comic name Varvara Nedotyopina (Barbara Left-in-the-Lurch): *nedotyopa* eventually became the catchphrase of old Firs.[1]

As it eventually took shape, *The Cherry Orchard* opens with a return and ends with a departure. Lyubov Ranevskaya's homecoming from Paris brings together on the family estate a cluster of characters attached to her by family or sentimental ties: her brother Gayev, her foster-daughter Varya, her daughter Anya, Trofimov the tutor to her dead son, various servants and hangers-on. Chief among them is Lopakhin, a former serf turned millionaire, who hopes to save the bankrupt estate by convincing its highborn owners to convert it into building lots for summer cottages. Gayev, however, is repelled by the vulgarity of the idea, and Ranevskaya refuses to accept the imminence of the estate's loss. On the very day of the auction-sale, she throws a party, which is interrupted by Lopakhin's triumphant announcement that the estate was knocked down to him. With the breakup of the old homestead, the characters scatter to different fates: Ranevskaya goes back to Paris, Gayev drifts into a bank job, Anya and Trofimov join their lives to work for the future good of mankind. In a final attempt to propose marriage to Varya, Lopakhin evades the issue, condemning her to be a spinster housekeeper. After they have all disappeared, only Firs, the superannuated retainer, is left to haunt the premises, a forgotten remnant of the past, as the first blows of the axe are heard in the orchard.

Chekhov stressed the comic nature of the play even as he wrote it: 'My play . . . hasn't turned out as a drama, but as a comedy, at times almost a farce' (to Olga Knipper, 15 Sept. 1903), and again, 'The last act will be gay. In fact the whole play is light and gay' (to Olga Knipper, 21 Sept. 1903). Misunderstandings arose as soon as the Moscow Art Theatre received the text. Nemirovich-Danchenko warned of an excess of tears (to Chekhov, 18 Oct. 1903), and Stanislavsky upset the author by insisting that 'this isn't a comedy or a farce as you wrote me, it's a tragedy, despite the sort of outlet towards a better life you foresee in the last act' (to Chekhov, 20 Oct. 1903). Chekhov responded with an explicit denial.

> Why do you say in your telegram that my play is full of tears? Where are they? Only Varya, Varya alone, by her very nature, is a crybaby, and her tears must not promote a sense of sadness in the audience. You can often find in my plays the stage-direction 'through tears' but this points to the condition of the character and not the tears. (To Nemirovich-Danchenko, 21 Oct 1903)

Throughout the rehearsals in Moscow, Chekhov tried hard from Yalta to prevent what he considered Stanislavsky's excesses. When the director asked to have sound effects of a passing train, frogs and thrushes in Act Two, Chekhov headed him off: 'Haymaking goes on about June 20 and or 25, I think by then the thrush has stopped singing, the frogs more or less shut up. Only the oriole is left . . . If you could present the train without any noise, without a single sound, go to it . . .' (to Stanislavsky, 23 Nov. 1903). The production was acclaimed as one of the MAT's more evocative, but Chekhov was unconvinced. The reports of friends that Stanislavsky dragged through the last act, prolonging it by thirty minutes, drove the author to cry, 'Stanislavsky has massacred my play!' (to Olga Knipper, 29 Mar 1904) and he was querulous that the posters and advertisements subtitled it a 'drama'. 'Nemirovich and Stanislavsky actually see something in the play other than what I wrote and I can swear the two of them have never once read my play attentively.'

Even if some of Chekhov's complaints can be dismissed as side-effects of his physical deterioration, there is no doubt that the Art Theatre staging misplaced many of Chekhov's intended emphases. He seems to have meant the major role to be Lopakhin, played by Stanislavsky. But Stanislavsky, the son of a textile manufacturer, preferred the part of the feckless aristocrat Gayev to that of a *nouveau riche*, and handed Lopakhin over to Leonidov, a less experienced actor. Olga Knipper, whom the author saw in the grotesque role of the German governess, was cast as Ranevskaya. Immediately the central focus shifted to the genteel family of landowners, because the strongest actors were in those parts. Later on, fugitives from the Revolution identified so closely with Ranevskaya and Gayev that they disseminated a nostalgic view of the gentry's plight throughout the West. Soviet productions then went to the opposite extreme, reinterpreting Lopakhin as a man of the people capable of building a new society, preferably by Five Year Plans, and the student Trofimov as an eloquent harbinger of that brave new world.

Choosing sides immediately reduces the play's complexity and ambiguity. Chekhov had no axe to grind, not even the one that hews down the orchard. Neither Lopakhin nor Trofimov is endowed with greater validity than Ranevskaya or Gayev. Trofimov is consistently undercut by comic devices: after a melodramatic exit line, 'All is over between us!', he falls downstairs, and, despite his claim to be in the vanguard of progress, is too absent-minded to locate his own galoshes, an undignified prop if ever there was one. Even his earnest speech about the idle upperclasses and the benighted workers is addressed to the wrong audience: how can Ranevskaya possibly identify with the Asiatic bestiality that Trofimov indicts as a Russian characteristic? Only in the hearing of infatuated Anya do Trofimov's words seem prophetic; at other times, his inability to realise his situation renders them absurd.

Chekhov was anxious to avoid the stage clichés of the *kulak*, the hard-hearted, loudmouthed merchant, in his portrayal of Lopakhin; after all, Lopakhin shares Chekhov's own background as a man of peasant origin who worked his way up in a closed society. He can be the tactless boor that Gayev insists he is, exulting over his purchase of the orchard and starting its decimation even before the family leaves. But in the same breath, he is aware of his shortcomings, longs for a more poetic existence, and has, in the words of his antagonistic Trofimov, 'delicate gentle fingers, like an artist . . . a delicate, gentle soul'. And for all his pragmatism, he too is comically inept when it comes to romance. His half-hearted wooing of Varya may result from a more deep-seated love of her foster-mother.

Ironically, it is the impractical Ranevskaya who pricks Lopakhin's dreams of giants and vast horizons and suggests that he examine his own grey life rather than build castles in the air. She may be an incorrigible romantic about the orchard and totally scatter-brained about money, but on matters of sex she is more clear-sighted than Lopakhin,

Anton Chekhov

Trofimov, or Gayev who brands her as 'depraved.' Prudish as a young Komsomol, Trofimov is as scandalised by her advice that he take a mistress, as he had been annoyed that Varya should distrust his moments alone with Anya.

In short, any attempt to grade Chekhov's characters as 'right-thinking' or 'wrong-headed' ignores the multi-faceted nature of their portrayal. It would be a mistake to adopt wholeheartedly either the sentimental attitude of Gayev and Ranevskaya to the orchard or the pragmatic and 'socially responsible' attitude of Lopakhin and Trofimov. By 1900 there was any number of works about uprooted gentlefolk and estates confiscated by *arrivistes*, including several plays by Ostrovsky. Pyotr Nevezhin's *Second Youth* (1883), a popular melodrama dealing with the breakup of an aristocratic clan, held the stage till the Revolution, and Chekhov had seen it. That same year Nikolay Solovyov's *Liquidation* appeared, in which an estate is saved by a rich peasant marrying the daughter of the family. Chekhov would not have been raking over these burnt-out themes, if he did not have a fresh angle on them. *The Cherry Orchard* is the play in which Chekhov most successfully achieved a 'new form', the amalgam of a symbolist outlook with the appurtenances of social comedy.

Perhaps A. R. Kugel was on the right track when he wrote, 'All the inhabitants of *The Cherry Orchard* are children and their behaviour is childish'.[2] Certainly, Chekhov seems here to have abandoned his usual reper-tory company: there is no doctor, no mooning *intelligent* complaining of a wasted life (Yepikhodov the autodidact may be a parody of the superfluous man), no love triangles (except the comic one of Yepikhodov-Dunyasha-Yasha). The only pistol is wielded by the hapless dolt Yepikhodov, and Nina's mysterious enveloping 'talma' in *The Seagull* has dwindled into Dunyasha's *talmochka*, a fancy term for a shawl, which she sends him on a fool's errand to fetch. Soliloquies have been replaced by monologues which are patently ridiculous (Gayev's speeches to the bookcase and the sunset) or misdirected (Trofimov's speech on progress). Simeonov-Pishchik, with his absurd name (something like 'Fitzwarren-Tweet'), his 'dear daughter Dashenka,' and his rapid mood shifts would be out of place in *Three Sisters*. The upstart valet Yasha, who smells of chicken-coops and patchouli, recalls Chichikov's servant Petrushka in *Dead Souls* who permeates the ambience with his effluvium. Gogol, rather than Turgenev, is the presiding genius of this comedy.

The standard theme of New or Roman comedy, the source of modern domestic drama, is that of the social misfit – miser or crank or misanthrope – creating a series of problems for young lovers. Confounded by a crafty servant who, under the aegis of comedy's holiday spirit, oversteps his rank, the misfit is either reintegrated into society or expelled from it. The result is an affirmation of society's ideals and conventions. By the late eighteenth century, this formula was beginning to break down: in Beaumarchais' *Marriage of Figaro*, the clever servant finds his master's aims too much in conflict with his own. The dissolution of the social fabric is prefigured by the growing tensions within the comic framework.

The Cherry Orchard carries forward this dissolution. All the characters are misfits, from Lopakhin who dresses like a rich man but feels 'like a pig in a pastry shop,' to Yasha and Dunyasha, servants who ape their betters, to the expelled student Trofimov ('Fate simply hustles me from place to place') to Yepikhodov who puts simple ideas into inappropriate language, to Varya who is a perfect manager but longs to be a pilgrim, to the most obvious example, the governess Charlotta, who has no notion who she is. Early

on, we hear Lopakhin protest, 'Have to know your place!'
Jean-Louis Barrault, the French actor and director, has
suggested that the servants are satiric reflections of their
master's ideals: old Firs is in the senescent flesh the roseate
past that Gayev waxes lyrical over; Yasha, that pushing
young particle, with his taste for Paris and champagne, is a
parody of Lopakhin's upward mobility; Trofimov's dreams
of social betterment and reading-rooms for workers are
mocked by Yepkihodov reading Buckle and beefing up his
vocabulary.[3]

If there is a norm here, it exists off-stage, in town, at the
bank, in the restaurant full of soap-smelling waiters, in
Mentone and Paris where Ranevskaya's lover pleads for
her return, or in Yaroslavl where Great-aunt frowns on the
family's conduct. Chekhov peoples this unseen world with
what Vladimir Nabokov might call 'homunculi.' In addition
to the lover and Auntie, there are Ranevskaya's alcoholic
husband and drowned son, Pishchik's daughter and the
Englishmen who find clay on his land, rich Deriganov who
might buy the estate, the Ragulins who hire Varya, the
famous Jewish orchestra, Gayev's deceased parents and
servants, the staff eating peas in the kitchen, and a host of
others to indicate that the cherry orchard is a desert island
in a teeming sea of life. Chekhov had used the device in
Uncle Vanya and *Three Sisters*, where Vanya's dead sister,
the prepotent Protopopov, Mrs Colonel Vershinin, and
Kulygin's headmaster shape the character's fates but are
never seen. In *The Cherry Orchard*, the plethora of
invisible beings fortifies the sense of the estate's vulnerabil-
ity, transience, and isolation.

Barrault also pointed out that 'the action' of the play is
measured by the outside pressures on the estate. In Act
One, the cherry orchard is in danger of being sold, in Act
Two it is on the verge of being sold, in Act Three it is sold,

and in Act Four it has been sold. The characters are defined by their responses to these 'events', which, because they are spoken of, intuited, feared, longed-for but never seen, automatically make the sale equivalent to Fate or Death in a play of Maeterlinck or Andreyev. As Henri Bergson insisted,[4] anything living that tries to stand still in fluid, evolving time becomes mechanical and thus comic. How do the characters take position in the temporal flow – are they retarded, do they move with it, do they try to outrun it? Those who refuse to join in (Gayev and Firs) or who rush to get ahead of it (Trofimov) can end up looking ridiculous.

Viewed as traditional comedy, *The Cherry Orchard* thwarts our expectations: the lovers are not threatened except by their own impotence (Lopakhin, Trofimov), the servants are uppish but no help to anyone (Yasha, Dunyasha), all the characters are expelled at the end, but their personal habits have undergone no reformation. Ranevskaya returns to her lover; Gayev, at his most doleful moment, pops another caramel into his mouth; Lopakhin and Trofimov are back on the road, one on business, the other on a mission. Even the abandonment of Firs hints that he cannot exist off the estate, but is, as Ranevskaya's greeting to him implied, a piece of furniture like 'my dear little table.' This resilience in the face of change, with the future yet to be revealed, is closest to the symbolist sense of human beings trapped in the involuntary processes of time, their own mortality insignificant within the broader current. A Bergsonian awareness that reality stands outside time, dwarfing the characters' mundane concerns, imbues Chekhov's comedy with its bemused objectivity.

It also bestows on *The Cherry Orchard* its oddly free-floating nature, the sense of persons suspended for the nonce. The present barely exists, elbowed aside by memory and nostalgia, on the one hand, and by expectation and hope on the other. When *The Cherry Orchard* first opened, the critic Nevedomsky remarked that the characters are simultaneously 'living persons, painted with the colours of vivid reality, and at the same schemata of that reality, as it were its foregone conclusions.'[5] Or as Kugel put it more succinctly, 'the inhabitants of *The Cherry Orchard* live, as if half asleep, spectrally, on the border-line of the real and mystical'.[6]

Chekhov's close friend, the writer Ivan Bunin, pointed out that there were no such cherry orchards to be found in Russia, that Chekhov was inventing an imaginary landscape.[7] The estate is a wasteland in which the characters drift among the trivia of their lives while expecting something dire or important to occur. As in Maeterlinck, the play opens with two persons waiting in a dimly-lit space, and closes with the imminent demise of a character abandoned in emptiness. Chekhov's favourite scenarios of waiting are specially attenuated here, since the suspense of 'What will happen to the orchard?' dominates the first three acts, and in the last act, the wait for carriages to arrive and effect the diaspora frames the conclusion.

But the symbolism goes hand-in-glove with carefully observed reality: they co-exist. According to the poet Andrey Bely, the instances of reality are scrutinised so closely in this play that one falls through them into a concurrent stream of 'eternity.' Hence the uneasiness caused by what seem to be humdrum characters or situations:

> How terrifying are the moments when Fate soundlessly sneaks up on the weaklings. Everywhere there is the alarming leitmotiv of thunder, everywhere the impending storm-cloud of terror. And yet, it would seem there's good reason to be terrified: after all, there's talk of

126

selling the estate. But terrible are the masks behind which the terror lurks, eyes goggling in the apertures.[8]

Act Two with its open-air setting demonstrates this concurrence of reality and super-reality. Chekhov's people are seldom at ease in the open. The more egoistic they are, like Arkadina and Serebryakov, the sooner they head for the safe haven of a house or, like Natasha, renovate nature to suit their taste. The last act of *Three Sisters* literally strands its protagonists in an uncongenial vacancy, with halloos echoing across the expanse.

By removing the characters in *The Cherry Orchard* from the memory-laden atmosphere of the nursery (where children should feel at home), Chekhov strips them of their defenses. In Act Two the characters meet on a road, one of those indeterminate locations, halfway between the station and the house, but symbolically, halfway between past and future, birth and death, being and nothingness. Something here impels them to deliver characteristic monologues: Charlotta complains of her lack of identity, Yepikhodov declares his suicidal urges, Ranevskaya describes her 'sinful' past, Gayev addresses the sunset, Trofimov speechifies on what's wrong with society, Lopakhin paints his hopes for Russia. As if hypnotised by the sound of their voices reverberating in the wilderness, they deliver up quintessences of themselves.

At this point comes the portentous moment of the snapped string:

Everyone sits down, absorbed in thought. The only sound is FIRS, softly muttering. Suddenly, a distant sound is heard, as if from the sky, the sound of a snapped string, dying away mournfully.
LYUBOV ANDREEVNA: What's that?

LOPAKHIN: I don't know. Somewhere far off in a mineshaft a bucket dropped. But somewhere very far off.

GAYEV: Or perhaps it was some kind of bird . . . such as a heron.

TROFIMOV: Or an owl.

LYUBOV ANDREEVNA *shivers*. Unpleasant anyway. *Pause*.

The moment is punctuated by those pauses that evoke the gaps in existence that Bely claimed were horrifying and that Beckett was to characterise as the transitional zone in which being made itself heard. Chekhov's characters again recall Maeterlinck's, faintly trying to surmise the nature of the potent force that hovers just outside the picture. The thought-filled pause, then the uncanny sound, and the ensuing pause conjure up what is beyond.

But even then, Chekhov does not forgo a realistic pretext for the inexplicable. Shortly before the moment, Yepikhodov crosses upstage, strumming his guitar. Might not the snapped string be one broken by the faltering bookkeeper? At the play's end, before we hear the sound plangently dying away, we are told by Lopakhin that he has left Yepikhodov on the grounds as a caretaker. Chekhov always overlays any symbolic inference with a patina of irreproachable reality.

The spell of the snapped string is broken by a tramp, chanting snatches of social protest poetry about the homeless poor. This allusion to their own essential rootlessness gives the characters a landfall for their formless fears, transferring the glimpse into the abyss to a more familiar plane.

The party scene in Act Three is the *locus classicus* of Chekhov's intermingling of subliminal symbol and surface reality. Bely saw it as 'a crystallisation of Chekhov's devices':

> In the foreground room a domestic drama is taking place; while, at the back, candle-lit, the masks of terror are dancing rapturously; there's the postal clerk waltzing with some girl – or is he a scarecrow? Perhaps he is a mask fastened to a walking-stick or a uniform hung on a clothes-tree. What about the stationmaster? Where are they from, what are they for? It is all an incarnation of fatal chaos. There they dance and simper as the domestic calamity comes to pass.[9]

The scene struck the imagination of the young director Meyerhold, who wrote to Chekhov (8 May 1904) that 'the play is abstract like a symphony by Tchaikovsky . . . in (the party scene) there is something Maeterlinckian, terrifying,' and he later referred to 'this nightmarish dance of puppets in a farce' in 'Chekhov's new mystical drama'.[10]

The act takes place in three dimensions: the forestage with its brief interchanges by individual characters, the forced gaiety of the dancing in the background, and the offstage auction whose outcome looms over it all. Without leaving the sphere of the mundane, we have what Novalis called 'a sequence of ideal events running parallel to reality'. Characters are thrust out from the indistinct background and then return to it. Scantily identified, the postal clerk and the stationmaster surge forward, unaware of the main characters' inner lives, and make unwitting ironic comment. The stationmaster, for instance, recites Aleksey Tolstoy's orotund poem 'The Sinful Woman' about a courtesan's conversion by the Christus at a lavish orgy in Judaea. The opening lines, describing a sumptuous banquet, cast a sardonic reflection on the frumps gathered on this dismal occasion. They also show the subsequent interview between the puritanical Trofimov ('I am above love') and the self-confessed sinner Ranevskaya to be a parodic confrontation between a Messiah with a scanty beard and a Magdalene in a Parisian ballgown. Charlotta is described in the stage directions as a nameless 'figure in a grey tophat and checked trousers' that waves its arms and jumps up and down, an unexplained phantasm erupting out of nowhere, just as Anya materialises behind a rug. (Charlotta's tricks, performed irrelevantly throughout the play, point up the arbitrariness of human action.) The act culminates in the moving juxtaposition of Ranevskaya's weeping and Lopakhin's laughter, as the unseen musicians play loudly at his behest.

A party as a playground for contrasting moods was a staple of romantic stagecraft. Surviving examples in Verdi's operas *Un Ballo in Maschera* and *La Traviata* (which might be translated *The Sinful Woman*) drew on popular plays by Scribe and Dumas *fils*. The Russian dramatic tradition was also rich in such situations: in *Woe from Wit*, Griboyedov scored the hectic tempo of the hero's despair against the inanity of a high society soirée; Pushkin's *Feast in Plaguetime* mordantly contrasted libertinage and fatality; Lermontov's *Masquerade* made a costume ball the setting for betrayal and murder. Chekhov's innovation is to reduce the romantic element to banality in consonance with his own favoured method. So the ball in *The Cherry Orchard* is a sorry congregation of provincial nobodies, upstart servants and a *klezmer* band. The gaiety becomes even more hollow and the pervasion of the grotesque more pungent.

The return to the nursery, now stripped of its evocative trappings, in Act Four, confirms the inexorable expulsion. In Act One, it had been a room to linger in; now it is a cheerless space in which characters loiter only momentarily on their way to somewhere else. The old Russian tradition of sitting for a moment before taking leave becomes especially meaningful when there are no chairs, only trunks and bundles to perch on. The champagne is going flat. The ghosts that Gayev and Ranevskaya had seen in the orchard in the first act have now moved indoors, in the person of Firs, who is doomed to haunt the scene of the past, since he has no future.

'Ladies in white dresses' had been one of Chekhov's earliest images for the play. Visually, the dominant note is etoliation, from Ranevskaya confusing the clusters of white blossoms in the garden with her late mother in a white dress, to the final tableau of Firs in his white waistcoat recumbent on the sofa. Achromatism is ambivalent: it is vernal and virginal, and at the same time the hue of dry bones and sterility. The white is set in relief by Varya's customary suit of woe. The American actress Eva Le Gallienne, astutely noted Chekhov's repetitive use of a young woman in black. 'Just as in painting there is a note of black in one of his female characters . . . the wearing of black is an outward manifestation of an inner state of mind, especially when worn by young women.'[11] *The Seagull*'s Masha, 'in mourning for her life,' and Masha in *Three Sisters* wearing black on a festive occasion, are shown up as poseuses. Varya fancies herself tramping the country from shrine to shrine, 'like a nun,' says Ranevskaya; but at the belt of her black gown hangs a ring of keys, the emblem of a bustling, officious nature ill-suited for spiritual withdrawal. When she gives up her keys, it is to fling them, in unholy anger, at Lopakhin.

The black and white of impending death tinge life at every turn, but without painting over the comic tonality. Act One is rife with *memento mori*: Lopakhin's 'late father' heads a cortege composed of Ranevskaya's mother, little

Grisha, the dead nanny and the dim Anastasy recollected by Gayev. 'I'm so glad you're still alive,' Ranevskaya says to Firs. But these obituaries are tossed off, not taken to heart; even Ranevskaya's aggrieved recollection of her dead past is cut off by the merry music of the Jewish orchestra. Finally, Charlotta mocks the pervasive sterility by nursing a baby made out of an empty parcel. The most touching eulogy is pronounced by the clownish Pishchik over himself.

The consummate mastery of *The Cherry Orchard* is revealed in an authorial shorthand that is both impression-istic and theatrical. The pull on Ranevskaya to return to Paris takes shape in the telegram prop: in Act One, she tears up the telegrams; by Act Three, she has preserved them in her handbag; in Act Four, the lodestones draw her back. The dialogue is similarly telegraphic, as in Anya's short speech relating how she found her mother in Paris: 'Mama was living on a fifth floor, I go upstairs, with her there are some French people, ladies, some old Catholic priest with a little book, and it's smoky, tawdry'. In a few strokes, a past is encapsulised: a high storey, bespeaking Ranevskaya's reduced circumstances, her toying with religious conversion, the *louche* atmosphere full of cigarette smoke.

Each character is distinguished by an appropriate speech pattern. Lyubov Ranevskaya (whose first name means 'love') constantly employs diminutives and terms of endearment; for her everyone is *golubchik*, 'dovie'. She is also vague, using adjectives like 'some kind of' (*kakoy-to*), suggestive of her passive nature. Gayev is a parody of the after-dinner speaker: emotion can be voiced only in a fulsome oration, thick with platitude. When his flow is staunched, he falls back on billiard terms or, like a Freudian baby arrested at the oral stage, stops his mouth with

132

caramels, anchovies and Kerch herrings. An untoward situation prompts him to say not 'What?' (*Chto?*) but the more effete 'How's that?' (*Chego?*)

Pishchik, always waiting, like Micawber, for something to turn up, has high blood pressure; so Chekhov the doctor makes sure he speaks in short, breathless phrases, a hodgepodge of old-world courtesy, hunting terms, and newspaper talk. Lopakhin's language is more varied, according to his addressee; blunt and colloquial with servants, more respectful with his former betters. As a businessman, his language is concise and well-structured, except when dealing with Vorya, when he lapses into a bleat: 'Me-e-eh.' He cites exact numbers and uses a commercial vocabulary, and frequently consults his watch.

Trofimov, like Gayev, is fond of rhetoric, but his is a mélange of literary and political war-cries. The stirring phrase about a 'shining star, glowing there in the distance! Forward! No dropping behind, friends' is patched together from Pushkin, Pleshcheyev and the Decembrists. He waxes most poetical with Anya, whom Chekhov has speak in iambs. Yepikhodov invents a style all his own, dropping formal locutions into colloquial discourse.

Firs' speech is pithy and demotic: his laconic remarks always bring a situation back to earth. His particular tag, *Ekh, ty nedotyopa* long bemused commentators. Some thought *nedotyopa* to be an obscure peasant word collected by Chekhov in the country; others believed he made it up. Translators have rendered it as everything from 'lummox' 'duffer' 'joblot' and 'good-for-nothing' to 'silly young cuckoo'. Literally, it means something in the process of being chopped by an axe, but left unfinished: perhaps 'half-baked' comes closest in English.

Memorably, 'Ah, you're half-baked' is the last line in the play. Its regular repetition suggests that Chekhov meant it to sum up all the characters. Like the chopping left undone, they are inchoate, some, like Anya and Trofimov, in the process of taking shape, others, like Gayev and Yepikhodov, never to take shape. The whole play has been held in a similar state of contingency until the final moments, when real chopping begins in the orchard and, typically, it is heard from offstage, mingled with the more cryptic and reverberant sound of the snapped string.

9
The Theatrical Filter

All one needs is your name on the poster – and there's a full house, and the actors pull themselves together: they treat each of your phrases, every word, with real reverence and don't allow themselves a single omission. *The provincial director I. A. Rostovtsev to Chekhov, 1900*

Chekhov's art is allusive, syncretic, rich in ambivalence: his standard practice when rewriting was to excise lines that seemed tautological or overly explicit. Stanislavsky's view of art was more Victorian: he meant it to illustrate, inform, and explain. In addition, Nemirovich-Danchenko emphasised the social purpose of drama. Consequently, a Moscow Art Theatre production treated a play not so much as the imaginative fruits of an individual author's sensibility as a segment of real experience, to be probed in depth. Because Chekhov's plays are grounded in reality and his characters are accretions of closely-observed psychological detail, the Moscow Art Theatre approach yielded successful results, but the success was only partial. Contemporary audiences

135

of intelligentsia were enthralled to see themselves and their malaise reflected with such authenticity, yet Chekhov felt, with some justice, that his reticence, ambiguities, and comic pacing were lost in the process. The Moscow Art Theatre rendered photographically what had been meant as pointillism.

In his director's book for *The Seagull*, Stanislavsky noted that a laugh offstage coming in the last act after Nina's quotation from Turgenev would be 'a vulgar effect.' But he could not resist it, because it was effective, and so it remained. Stanislavsky's whole approach to directing was to erect signposts to explicit meaning, and translate ambiguity into easily apprehended stage messages. Ultimately the Art Theatre's greatest gift to Chekhov was its insistence on ensemble playing, or in Stanislavsky's words, 'today Hamlet, tomorrow a walk-on'. Since Chekhov's casts are integral units, unstratified into leading characters and *comprimario* roles, he could be most faithfully performed by a company that devoted as much time to creating an inner life for Ferapont as it would for Vershinin.

This became clear when Chekhov's plays entered the repertory of other theatres. At the State-subsidised Alexandra in St. Petersburg, when the characters began to dance at the Shrovetide party in *Three Sisters*, Davydov, who played Chebutykin, came downstage centre and performed a Cossack dance as a music-hall turn, to audience applause.[1] Such was the custom, even in realistic drama. Under these circumstances, even if the Art Theatre somewhat distorted Chekhov, he was fortunate that it existed to launch his plays in a far less compromised form that they might otherwise have assumed. The Moscow Art Theatre style was copied by provincial theatres, and became the model for producing Chekhov, even in China and Japan.

Chekhov left no school. The poet Aleksandr Blok specifically stated that 'he had no precursors, and his successors do not know how to do anything *à la* Chekhov'. 'Lyricism is especially prevalent in Chekhov's plays,' he continued, 'but his mysterious gift was not passed on to anyone else, and his innumerable imitators have given us nothing of value.'[2] One of those who tried to perpetuate Chekhov's so-called lyricism was Boris Zaytsev, whose *The Lanin Estate* was put on by a group of students under the leadership of Stanislavsky's favourite disciple Yevgeny Vakhtangov in 1914. Audiences of the eve of Revolution found it an irrelevant threnody.

After the Revolution, Chekhov went out of fashion in Russia, for his plays too were dismissed as irrelevant to Soviet society. Along with the Moscow Art Theatre, they were condemned as relics of an obsolete bourgeois way of life, appealing only to the same ineffectual types that peopled his drama. The leftist poet Mayakovsky, in a prologue to his agit-prop play *Mystery-Bouffe*, sneered, You go to the theatre and 'You look and see/ – Auntie Manyas and Uncle Vanyas flopping on divans./ Neither uncles nor aunts interest us,/ We can get uncles and aunts at home'.[3] Another complaint was that Chekhov was too pessimistic at a time when 'active progressivism' was the byword. By the 1930s, only the vaudevilles and *The Cherry Orchard* were revived, with Trofimov and Lopakhin exalted as heralds of the Revolution.

Consequently, the two greatest directors of this period turned to the farces when they directed Chekhov. Vakhtangov prepared an evening of one-acts, *The Wedding*, *The Jubilee*, and a dramatisation of the short story 'Thieves' for the Moscow Art Theatre Third Studio in 1920, reviving them at his own theatre the next year. His work began with the question, 'How are we going to portray Chekhov's characters, are we to defend them or condemn them?' Essentially, he chose the latter course, and, in *The Wedding*, the characters were portrayed as a collection of vulgar grotesques. Only the 'General' contributed warmth and cheer, and when he rushed out crying 'Chelove-e-ek! Chelove-e-ek!' (both 'Man' and 'Waiter!') the audience was so shattered it could not applaud. The author's nephew Michael Chekhov who had guffawed throughout could, at this final curtain, whisper only 'What a horror! What a horror!'[4]

Vsevolod Meyerhold as a tyro director had staged facsimiles of the Moscow Art Theatre productions in the provinces and did not return to Chekhov until 1935, the 75th anniversary of the playwright's birth. Then he presented three farces, *The Jubilee*, *The Bear*, and *The Proposal*, under the collective title *33 Swoons*, computed by Meyerhold to be the number of fainting-fits that occur in the plays. To the cast, he announced that these swoons constituted the leit-motivs of the performance, a series of theatrical games; to the world at large, he proclaimed that the swoons exemplified the neurasthenic legacy of the pre-Revolutionary intelligentsia. Overcharged with innumerable props, complicated pantomime and sight gags, the vaudevilles proved broadly funny at times, but were condemned by critics for directorial exhibitionism and heavy-handedness.

The first important re-interpretation of Chekhov in Russia came from Nemirovich-Danchenko. Directing a *Cherry Orchard* in Milan (1933) with an Italian troupe headed by the emigrée actress Tatiana Pavlova, Nemirovich was able to discard some Moscow Art Theatre traditions and bring Ranevskaya and Trofimov closer to what he believed had been Chekhov's intention. Returning to Russia, he set about to revitalise *Three Sisters*, whose characters he saw not as futile and trivial, but as fine minds 'longing for life,' fit to be acted in a style of 'virile strength.'[5] Everything from uniforms to dressing-gowns was made beautiful, everything cold or degrading was eliminated. The sisters became a musical trio, set off against the raucous Natasha (Stanislavsky's wife Lilina had played Natasha as sickly sweet; here A. Georgievskaya made her a monster of crassness). The final hymn to the future was performed without Chebutykin's ironic counterpoint.

The French director, Michel Saint-Denis, who saw this 'affirmative' revision in 1940, remarked

> It was a production of a very high standard, but it was Chekhov simplified both in style and meaning. The simplification of the out-of-door set for the last act was welcome but lacked unity. The play had been speeded up in tempo . . . The poetic values had been damaged in favour of a more optimistic, more clearly constructive meaning. Nostalgic melancholy, even despair, had given way to positive declarations.[6]

Chekhov underwent another eclipse in the Soviet Union during the Great Patriotic War, and not until 1944 did *The Seagull* receive an innovative production. Aleksandr Tairov, the waning director of the Kamerny (Chamber) Theatre, staged it as a concert reading, with a sound Marxist line that man's capability could overcome all obstacles through belief in his own potential. Nina, played by his wife Alisa Koonen, thus became the leading character.

A more influential breakthrough was made by Georgy Tovstonogov's *Three Sisters* at the Bolshoy Dramatic Theatre in Leningrad (1965), which found a way to bring out the play's contemporaneity without discarding the

Moscow Art Theatre model entirely. His designer, S. Iunovich, kept to a black-white-grey palette and provided stage islands which jutted out into the audience to create the theatrical equivalent of the 'close-up' for a public brought up on movies. The tone of the production was epic, showing the wind of history blowing through the characters' lives, their hopes shattered by the passage of time.

The *enfant terrible* of Russian Chekhov directors has been Anatoly Efros, who stirred up a terrific controversy in 1966 with his *The Seagull* at the Lenin–Komsomol Theatre in Moscow. It emphasised two typical post-war themes: idealistic youth having to compromise with adult life, and the incompatibility of talent with fakery. V. Smirnitsky's Treplyov was active, restless and childlike, the nexus of the play; while the rest of the characters, adrift and frustrated, were nasty to each other in a vicious, strident manner. This note was struck more loudly in Efros's *Three Sisters* (Malaya Bronnaya Theatre, Moscow, 1967), a staging without half-tones: every petty grievance exploded into a loud quarrel or scandal. Motivation was, as a rule, sexual: Natasha had needs which frigid Andrey could not meet, so she was justified in taking a lover; Irina was a capricious *demi-vierge*, Masha a coarse predator, Olga repressed and repressive. Efros came back to Chekhov in 1975 with an iconoclastic *The Cherry Orchard* (Taganka, Moscow): the unit set suggested a graveyard hemmed in by billowing window-curtains and family portraits. The characters were seen as highstrung neurotics, an increasingly popular notion with contemporary Soviet directors.

This tendency came to a head in the Taganka's *Three Sisters* directed by Yury Lyubimov. The play began by sliding open a wall of the theatre to reveal a military band and the Moscow street outside the building; when closed, the wall's mirrored surface threw the audience's image back in its face. This opening statement more than hinted that the sisters' plight was a contemporary one with existential overtones. The characters, isolated from one another, wandered desolately about until they banged into the sheet-metal wall engraved with iconic figures. Such extreme re-interpretations of Chekhov were meaningful when set against the Moscow Art Theatre tradition. Russian critics and spectators could savour and analyse the divagation from the orthodox renditions. Most often, they would condemn it as wilfully perverse; occasionally, they would welcome a new revelation of meaning.

A recent adaptation of Chekhov's themes to modern Soviet life is Vladimir Arro's *Look Who's Come* (1982), in which a famous writer's widow resolves to sell his dacha to a troika of vulgarians: a hairdresser, a bartender and a bathhouse attendant. Despite good reviews and responsive audiences, the government forced the author to alter the ending: the suicide of a dacha resident was replaced by the *deus ex machina* of a phone call, cancelling the sale. Soviet censorship prefers its Chekhovs to deal in happy endings.

In the English-speaking world, Chekhov's acceptance was not immediate, though now he has attained the status of a classic: no respectable repertory theatre considers itself fully fledged until it has tested itself in one of his four masterpieces. During the course of this assimilation, Chekhov received some enduring and often misleading interpretations. First taken to be a purveyor of gloom and doom, he has, as Spencer Golub notes, 'been ennobled by age . . . He is as soothing and reassuring as the useless valerian drops dispensed by the doctors in his plays . . . an article of faith, like all stereotypes . . . the Santa Claus of dramatic literature . . .'[7] How this falsely benign image took shape is worth examining.

British productions got off to a good start with *The*

Seagull at the Glasgow Repertory Theatre (November 1908). Its translator and director, the knowledgeable George Calderon, declared that 'a play of Tchekhof is a reverie, not a concatenation of events'; insistent that Chekhov's plays went beyond mere naturalism, he stressed what reviewers deemed the play's 'Ibsenite symbolism'.[8] He also compensated for British actors' inability to maintain an inner life when not speaking lines, by stressing the transitions between group mood and individual reactions. The result was impressive.

Unfortunately, the first London Chekhov was less propitious. Its sponsor, George Bernard Shaw, characterised the Stage Society *Cherry Orchard* (1911) as 'the most important [opening] in England since that of *A Doll's House*'.[9] But the Stage Society was primed for social messages and dramas of reform; it and its public were baffled by the characters' self-involvement and assumed that the play was an emanation of some mythical Slavic soul. They judged it against the standard of the well-made problem play, and took Lopakhin to be a brutish villain, the Gayev family charming victims and Yepikhodov as the 'raisonneur'. Shaw felt compelled to adopt the Chekhovian ethos to his own messianic ends in *Heartbreak House* (1919). It was not until after the Great War that British audiences discovered a rapport with Chekhov.

The mood of embittered disillusionment that followed the War suddenly made the yearnings and fecklessness of Chekhov's people seem apposite, at the same time that the literary avant-garde was popularising his stories. His plays were greeted as contemporary dejection in Russian dress. Another agent in this naturalisation process was the emigré director Theodore Komisarjevsky (Fyodor Kommissarzhevsky) who mounted a series of Chekhov productions between 1925 and 1936, far better integrated and skilfully acted than any previously seen. They employed winning young players such as John Gielgud, Charles Laughton, Edith Evans and Peggy Ashcroft, with whom audiences could empathise. Komisarjevsky had no qualms about cutting the plays and skewing them to bring out the more mawkish aspects. Gielgud relates of the 1926 *Three Sisters* (Barnes Theatre):

> The play was dressed in 1880s costumes, and Tusenbach, shorn of his lines about his ugliness, was played (by Komisarjevsky's express direction) as a romantic juvenile . . . When I questioned him about the 'ugly' lines being cut, he shrugged his expressive shoulders and said, 'My dear boy, the English public always demand a love interest.'[10]

These productions promoted in the English mind an image of Chekhov as pastel-coloured, moonstruck and sentimental. Epigones like Rodney Ackland and N. C. Hunter in their plays tried to transplant the seemingly fragile exotic to a familiar landscape of Bloomsbury boarding-houses and Dorset manors, with only partial success. Still, for the actor, Gielgud recalled, 'playing Chekhov in the twenties and thirties was to us like discovering a new form . . .'[11]

The actor-oriented productions of this period culminated in Tyrone Guthrie's *The Cherry Orchard* at the Old Vïc with Laughton as Lopakhin and Athene Seyler as Ranevskaya (1933); and a *Three Sisters* (Queen's Theatre, 1938), directed by Michel Saint-Denis, founder of the Compagnie des Quinze. Its superb cast, including Michael Redgrave as Tusenbach, was recollected by many as one of the most perfect examples of teamwork ever seen on the London stage. Given eight weeks to rehearse instead of the usual four, the actors were able to live into their roles to a remarkable degree: for the first time, an English audience was seeing an indigenous company approximate the Moscow Art Theatre.

Laurence Olivier played Astrov in a respected *Uncle Vanya* at the New Theatre in 1945, with Ralph Richardson in the title part; he returned to the role in 1962 at the Chichester Festival, this time yoked with Redgrave. The most original aspect of the production was its use of a unit set for all the acts. This made sense economically and technically, but played hob with Chekhov's symbolic progress from exterior to interior.

The average English Chekhovian production had become a stereotype, the languorous maundering of trivial people that Peter Ustinov parodied in *The Love of Four Colonels*, with army officers knitting in swings and *non sequitur* conversations stalling over unpronounceable names. Critics began to complain of the self-pity and the slow motion, that, in the words of one, supplied 'an invisible hassock for the reverential.'[12] Clearly, a fresh approach was called for. But British theatre kept the Komisarjevsky pattern well into the 1970s, relying more on strong individual performances than on a directorial overview.

New attitudes began to surface in Lindsay Anderson's *Seagull* (1975) which went overboard in its search for farce, and in the work of Jonathan Miller. As a physician, Miller shared Chekhov's clinical acumen, and in his *Seagull* (Chichester, 1974) he presented a nosology of the characters' symptoms. Treplyov's Oedipal complex was anatomised to a fare-thee-well, aided by Irene Worth's crooning a lullaby as she bandaged his head; and, in the last act, Sorin exhibited the effects of his stroke in his thickened speech. Miller's *Three Sisters* (Cambridge Theatre, 1976) undercut the usual romantic sympathy for the threesome, in an attempt to work against *idées reçus* about Chekhov.

A similar repudiation of the popular image was to be seen in *The Cherry Orchard* adapted by Trevor Griffiths, a playwright of socialist leanings (Nottingham, 1977), which dwelt on the social inequities among the characters and invested all its positive significance in Lopakhin as it dwelt on the social inequities among the characters. A more radical endeavour was Thomas Kilroy's transference of the action of *The Seagull* to *fin-de-siècle* Ireland (Royal Court Theatre, 1981). For many British playgoers, the social equation made great sense and brought the characters more clearly into focus. It also pointed up the jokes: when the Arkadina figure, Isobel Desmond, responded to her son's play by exclaiming, 'Good Lord, it's one of those Celtic things,' it brought down the house.

Chekhov was barely known on the American stage before the Moscow Art Theatre arrived on its tours of 1923–24, with a repertory including *Three Sisters*, *The Cherry Orchard*, *Uncle Vanya*, and *Ivanov*, in many cases with the actors who had originally created the roles. Although the Moscow Art Theatre itself regarded these productions as outmoded, they were eye-opening to American actors and playgoers. Despite the incomprehensible Russian dialogue, they were struck by the ensemble playing and the extra dimension Chekhov assumed when realised so thoroughly in every detail.

The earliest results of this epiphany could be seen in the work of Eva Le Gallienne for the Civic Repertory Theatre (1926–1933). The ambitions of Le Gallienne, an actress of wide culture and taste, usually outstripped her capabilities, for although she tried to emulate the Moscow Art Theatre's stage pictures and deliberate rhythms, her casts were mediocre (with the exception of Alla Nazimova as an

145

incandescent Ranevskaya); her productions were admirable more for good intentions than for exciting theatrics.

Chekhov was now viewed as good box-office if titivated with popular stars. The shrewd producer Jed Harris mounted an *Uncle Vanya* (1937) with Hollywood celebrity Lillian Gish as Yelena, and in 1938, Alfred Lunt and Lynn Fontanne lent their formidable talents to a production of Stark Young's spare new translation of *The Seagull.* It was of this staging that Noël Coward remarked, 'I hate a play with a dead bird sitting on the mantelpiece shrieking, "I'm the title, I'm the title, I'm the title" '.[13] The star-studding of Chekhov reached its apogee in Guthrie McClintic's *Three Sisters* (1942), with Katherine Cornell as Masha, Judith Anderson as Olga, Ruth Gordon as Natasha, and Edmund Gwenn as Chebutykin. The cast was of disparate backgrounds and training, and McClintic seemed to subscribe to the view that Chekhov's play was a sombre tragedy of three statuesque heroines downed by a middle-class Fury. The sluggish pace drove Stark Young to remark that 'Chekhov in performance in English nearly always suffers from what seems to be some sort of notion that thinking is slow . . .'[14]

After World War II, Americans tried to naturalise Chekhov by transferring his milieu to more familiar climes. *Platonov* became *Fireworks on the James* (Provincetown Playhouse, 1940) and *The Cherry Orchard* was transmogrified into Joshua Logan's *The Wisteria Trees* (Martin Beck Theatre, 1950), set in a post-bellum Southern plantation, with the servants former slaves, Lopakhin an enriched sharecropper, and Ranevskaya an ageing belle. American directors, when not aping Stanislavsky's alleged methods, went to grotesque extremes to be original, as in the APA's *The Seagull* of 1962, played in modern dress, with frozen tableaux and speeded-up action.

Paradoxically, American playwrights were steeped in

Chekhov and wrote a kind of poetic realism they hoped would match his. He had a direct influence on Clifford Odets and Irwin Shaw before the war; during the 1950s, Robert Anderson, William Inge, Arthur Miller, Lillian Hellman, Paddy Chayefsky and others testified to the power is his example. Miller confessed, 'I fairly worshipped Chekhov at an early time in my life . . . the depth of feeling in his work, its truthfulness and the rigor with which he hewed to the inner reality of his people are treasured qualities to me'.[15] But the actors and directors who were capable of brilliantly interpreting the works of these disciples found their technique inadequate to cope with the master himself.

The American theatre's deficiencies showed up most garishly in the long-awaited *Three Sisters* directed by Lee Strasberg for the Actor's Studio of New York, the Mecca of Method. Working with a galaxy of Studio alumni and veterans of the Group Theater, Strasberg, the self-proclaimed heir to Stanislavsky, proved to be a pedestrian director who gave line-readings and relied on runthroughs. The consequent performances were uncoordinated, wanting in pace, detail, and continuity, 'a formless, uninflected evening by the samovar'.[16]

The first real impetus to abrogating Stanislavsky's sovereignty came from Eastern Europe. In the West, a number of gifted directors – Georges Pitoëff, Jean-Louis Barrault, Giorgio Strehler, Luchino Visconti, Peter Zadek – had offered persuasive presentations of Chekhov without enunciating a new aesthetic. Informed by national traditions of fantastic allegory and satire, Eastern European directors broke through the fourth-wall illusion to present a colder, less psychologised ambience. The Czech Otomar Krejca was the first to discard the illusionistic box set for *The Seagull*, by having Josef Svoboda project impressionistic images on the back wall. The Rumanian Lucian Pintilie, working in France and the United States, surrounded his *Seagull* with gigantic mylar screens to illuminate the characters' narcissism, and made Treplyov's platform stage the central metaphor of the performance.

The Rumanian Andrei Serban has been the most controversial of these innovators, since much of his work has been done in the more conservative New York theatre. His *Cherry Orchard* (New York Publick Theatre, 1977) was filled with visual metaphors set against a luminous cyclorama: a cage-like ballroom; a plough dragged across a field by peasants; at the end, a cherry branch placed by a child in front of an enormous factory. 'All this is meant to elicit emotion rather than give information,' Serban explained.[17] The visual images were irreproachable and initiated a spate of imitative 'white-on-white' productions, but meaning was lost in farcical business and abrupt mood changes. Serban's later work included a *Seagull* in Japan (1980), centred around a magical lake; a more pedestrian *Seagull* in New York (1981); a *Three Sisters* (American Repertory Theatre, Cambridge, Mass 1983) that made a concerted effort to present the characters as a kindergarten of obnoxious brats; and an *Uncle Vanya* (La Mama, New York, 1983, with Joseph Chaikin as Vanya), notable for a cavernous set that kept the characters in isolation from one another. The consensus is that Serban, in exorcising the demon of Stanislavsky, has provided stunning imagery and provocative moments but not well-acted, coherent and cohesive readings.

Peter Brook, possibly the most prestigious director on the world scene, had in his influential book *The Empty Space* (1969) foresworn the notion that Chekhov created slices of life; rather, Brook said, he removed and cultured the *mille-feuille* layers of life 'in an exquisitely cunning,

completely artificial and meaningless order in which part of
the cunning lay in so disguising the artifice that the result
looked like the keyhole view it had never been'. More than
just an illusion of life, they are a 'series of alienations: each
rupture is a provocation and a call to thought.'[18]

Over a decade later, Brook embarked on his first
Chekhov production, *The Cherry Orchard* (Bouffes du
Nord, Paris, 1981) as 'a theatrical movement purely played
. . . From the start I wanted to avoid sentimentality, a false
Chekhovian manner that is not in the text'. Played in
French with an international cast, the accessories stripped
to a carpet, a few cushions and some straight-backed chairs
to prevent the essentials from being lost in a welter of
set-pieces, *The Cherry Orchard* became a poem about 'life
and death and transition and change.' 'While playing the
specifics,' Brook states, 'we also try to play the myth – the
secret play.'[19] Stanislavsky would have taken the 'secret
play' to be the *perezhivaniya*, inner emotional experiences,
ticking away in the pauses; Brook revealed a timelessness
in the situation, and, along the way, ensemble comedy that
did not need recourse to slapstick.

Like any densely textured dramatic work, Chekhov's
plays in production require both the unifying vision that
comes from a director and a company of strong actors,
melded together as a nuanced, quasi-musical entity. Realism alone has proven to be insufficient to convey what
George Calderon, as far back as 1912, called the 'cen-
trifugal' nature of Chekhov's dramas, which

> seek, not so much to draw our minds inwards to the
> consideration of the events they represent, as to cast
> them outwards to the larger process of the world which
> these events illuminate; . . . the sentiments to be aroused
> by the doings and sufferings of the personages of his

stage are not so much hope and fear for their individual
fortunes as pity and amusement at the importance they
set on them, and consolation for their particular
tragedies in the spectacle of the general comedy of Life in
which they are all merged . . .[20]

References

1. A Life

1. The date given by Chekhov himself, although he would appear to have been born on the 16th. The 17th was his 'name-day,' that is, the day of the saint for whom he was christened. Dates given here are 'Old Style,' in accord with the Julian calendar, twelve days behind the Gregorian.

2. M. P. Chekhov, *Vokrug Chekhova* (Moscow: Moskovsky rabochy, 1980), p. 44.

3. Ernest Simmons, *Chekhov. A Biography* (Boston: Little, Brown, 1962), p. 6.

4. Peter the Great had established a table of ranks which stratified society status into civil, military, naval and ecclesiastical hierarchies. In the civil hierarchy, *meshchanin* (townsman) came just above peasant. Treplyov, in *The Seagull*, complains that his father had been classified as a *meshchanin* of Kiev, even though he was a famous actor, and that the same rank appears on his own passport. He finds it particularly galling since the term had come to suggest petty bourgeois philistinism.

5. Letter to Dmitry Savlyev, Jan. (?) 1884. All quotations from Chekhov's creative writings and letters are based on the texts in A. P. Chekhov, *Polnoe sobranie sochineny i pisem* (30

vols.) (Moscow: Nauka, 1974–1974), henceforth referred to as PSS. Unless otherwise indicated, all translations are my own.

6. Maksim Gorky, *Literary Portraits*, tr. Ivy Litvinov (Moscow: Foreign Languages Publishing House, n.d.), pp. 158–59.

2. At The Play

1. V. F. Tretyakov, *Ocherki istori i Taganrogskogo teatra s 1827 do 1927 god* (Taganrog: Izd. Khud. Sektsii Taganrogskogo Okrolitrosveta, 1928), pp. 36–38.

2. PSS, III, 95.

3. PSS, V, 455.

4. PSS, XVI, 65.

5. M. P. Chekhov, *Vokrug Chekhova* (Moscow: Moskovsky rabochy, 1964), p. 212. All mention of Yavorskaya is dropped from the most recent edition.

6. PSS, XVI, 60.

7. M. P. Chekhov, *Vokrug Chekhova* (Moscow: Moskovsky rabochy, 1980), p. 142.

8. Dmitry Merezhkovsky, 'Neoromantizm v drame,' *Vestnik inostrannoy literatury* 11 (1894), p. 101.

9. Anton Krayny (pseud. of Zinaida Gippius), 'O poshlosti,' *Literaturny dnevnik (1899–1907)* (St. Petersburg: M. V. Pirozhkov, 1908), pp. 221–22.

10. Olga Knipper-Chekhova, 'Ob A. P. Chekhove,' *Vospominaniya i stati* (Moscow: Iskusstvo, 1972), I, 57.

11. Quoted by Arseny Gurlyand, 'Vospominaniya ob A. P. Chekhove,' *Teatr i iskusstvo* 28 (1904).

12. A. I. Urusov, *Stati yego o teatre, literature i iskusstve* (Moscow; Tip. I. N. Kholchev i ko., 1907), II, 34.

3. Journeyman Efforts

1. M. P. Chekhov, 'Ob A. P. Chekhove,' *Novoe slovo* 1 (1907), p. 198.

2. *Pisma A. P. Chekhovu yego brata Aleksandra Chekhova*, ed. I. S. Yezhov (Moscow: Gos. sotsialno-ekonomicheskoe izd., 1939), pp. 50–51.

3. Chekhov did not know the German's 'masochistic' works, but did see one of his plays.

References

4. A. R. Kugel, *Russkie dramaturgi* (Moscow: Mir, 1934), p. 33.

5. Letter to Chekhov from Pavel Svobodin (25 Oct. 1889), in *Chekhov i teatr*, ed. E. D. Surkov (Moscow: Iskusstvo, 1961), p. 211.

6. M. P. Chekhov, *Vokrug Chekhova* (Moscow: Moskovsky rabochy, 1980), p. 152.

7. Khrushchyov's nickname 'Leshy' gives too diabolic an impression when translated as 'Wood-Demon'; there is nothing Mephistophelian about the mischievous sprite which the ancient Slavs thought inhabited the forests. Russians use 'leshy voz'mi' the way an Englishman might say 'Deuce take it.' 'Wood-goblin' might be more appropriate.

8. A. P. Chudakov, *Chekhov's Poetics*, tr. F. J. Cruise and D. Dragt (Ann Arbor: Ardis, 1983), p. 210.

9. Quoted in D. Gorodetsky, 'Mezdu "Medvedem" i "Leshim",' *Birzhevye vedomosti* 364 (1904).

4. The One-Act Plays

1. Quoted in PSS, XI, 403.

2. Quoted in PSS, XI, 427.

3. A. S. Suvorin, *Tatyana Repina, komediya v chetyrakh deystvyakh* (St. Petersburg: A. S. Suvorin, 1889), Act IV, scene 3.

4. *Ibid.*, Act III, scene 6.

5. Quoted in PSS, XII, 397.

5. The Seagull

1. K. S. Stanislavsky, *My Life in Art*, tr. J. J. Robbins (Boston: Little, Brown, 1924), p. 355.

2. A. I. Urusov, *Stati yego o teatre, literature i iskusstve* (Moscow: Tip. I. N. Kolchev i ko., 1907), II, 35–38. First appeared in *Kuryer* (3 Jan. 1889).

3. A. G. Gladkov, 'Meyerhold govorit,' *Novy Mir* 8 (1961), p. 221.

4. Leonid Andreyev, 'Letters on the Theatre,' in *Russian Dramatic Theory from Pushkin to the Symbolists*, ed. and tr. L. Senelick (Austin: University of Texas Press, 1981), pp. 238–242.

5. A. N. Ostrovsky, *Artistes and Admirers*, tr. E. Hanson (Manchester: Manchester University Press, 1970), p. 64.

6. A. P. Chudakov, *Chekhov's Poetics*, tr. F. J. Cruise and D. Dragt (Ann Arbor: Ardis, 1983), p. 193.

7. D. S. Mirsky, *Contemporary Russian Literature 1881–1925* (London: George Routledge and sons, 1926), p. 88.

8. Nina's last name 'Zarechnaya' literally means 'on the other side of the river,' both suggestive of her alien status on the estate and reminiscent of *zamorskaya*, 'on the other side of the water,' a term frequently synonymous in Russian folklore with 'wondrous strange.'

9. W. B. Yeats, *The Collected Poems* (London and New York: Macmillan, 1964).

6. Uncle Vanya

1. 27 January 1899, quoted in S. S. Koteliansky, 'A note on "The Wood Demon"', in *The Wood Demon* (New York: Macmillan, 1926), p. 14.

2. M. Gorky and A. Chekhov, *Stati, vyskazyvaniya, perepiska* (Moscow: Goslitizdat, 1951), pp. 63–65.

3. Osip Mandelshtam, 'O pyese A. Chekhova "Dyadya Vanya," ' [1936] *Sobranie sochineny* 4 (Paris: YMCA Press), pp. 107–109.

4. Samuel Beckett, *Proust* (London: Chatto and Windus, 1931), p. 8.

5. Also the sub-title of Turgenev's *A Month in the Country*.

6. Chekhov may have had in mind the Russian fairy-tale of 'Yelena the Fair,' a Cinderella story in which the snivelling booby Vanya woos and wins the beautiful princess with the aid of his dead father. An English version can be found in *Russian Fairy Tales* by W. R. B. Ralston (London, 1887).

7. Robert Mazzocco, 'In Chekhov's spell,' *New York Review of Books* (22 Jan. 1976), p. 35.

8. Vsevolod Meyerhold, 'Teatre (k istorii tekhnike),' in *Teatr: kniga o novom teatre* (St. Petersburg: Shipovnik, 1908), pp. 143–45. A partial English translation of this essay appears in *Meyerhold on Theatre*, ed. and tr. Edward Braun (London: Methuen, 1969), pp. 25–39.

References

7. Three Sisters

1. Vladimir Ladyzhensky, 'Dalyokie gody,' *Rossiya i slavyanstvo* (13 July 1929), p. 5.
2. Olga Knipper-Chekhova, 'Ob A. P. Chekhove,' *Vospominaniya i stati* (Moscow: Iskusstvo, 1972), I, 56.
3. Maksim Gorky, *Sobranie sochineniya* (Moscow: Akademiya Nauk SSR, 1958), XXVIII, 159.
4. Leonid Andreyev, 'Tri sestry,' *Polnoe sobranie sochineny* (St. Petersburg: A. F. Marks, 1913), VI, 321–25.
5. Randall Jarrell, 'About *The Three Sisters*: Notes,' in *The Three Sisters* (London: Macmillan, 1969), pp. 105–106. There had been an impressionist show in Moscow in 1896, and Tolstoy had characterised Chekhov's technique as a story-writer as impressionism. As early as 1912 George Calderon was comparing *The Cherry Orchard* to a French 'vibrationist' picture.
6. Jovan Hristić, *Le théâtre de Tchékhov*, tr. H. and F. Wybrands (Lausanne: L'Age d'homme, 1982), p. 166.

8. The Cherry Orchard

1. Varya is another variant of the driven housekeeper-type Chekhov had described in his plans for a collaborative play with Suvorin. Earlier avatars include Yuliya in *The Wood Demon*, Sonya in *Uncle Vanya* and Natasha in *Three Sisters*.
2. A. R. Kugel, *Russkie dramaturgi* (Moscow: Mir, 1934), p. 120.
3. Jean-Louis Barrault, 'Pourquoi *La Cerisaie*?', *Cahiers de la Compagnie Barrault-Renaud* 6 (July 1954), pp. 87–97.
4. Henri Bergson, *Laughter, an Essay on the Meaning of the Comic*, tr. C. Brereton and F. Rothwell (New York, Macmillan, 1911), pp. 88–89.
5. M. Nevedomsky, 'Simvolizm v posledney drame A. P. Chekhova,' *Mir bozhy* 8, 2 (1904), pp. 18–19.
6. Kugel, *op. cit.*, p. 125.
7. Ivan Bunin, *O Chekhove* (New York: Chekhov Publishing House, 1955), p. 216.
8. Andrey Bely, 'The Cherry Orchard,' in *Russian Dramatic Theory from Pushkin to the Symbolists*, ed. and tr. L. Senelick (Austin: University of Texas Press, 1981), p. 92.

9. *Ibid.*

10. Vsevolod Meyerhold, *Perepiska* (Moscow: Iskusstvo, 1976), p. 45; and 'Teatr (k istorii tekhnike),' in *Teatr: kniga o novom teatre* (St. Petersburg: Shivpovnik, 1908), pp. 143–45.

11. Eva Le Gallienne, *At 33* (New York: Longmans, Green, 1934), p. 224.

9. The Theatrical Filter

1. Yu. M. Yuryev, *Zapiski* (Leningrad-Moscow: Iskusstvo, 1963), II, 135.

2. Aleksandr Blok, 'On Drama,' in *Russian Dramatic Theory from Pushkin to the Symbolists*, ed. and tr. L. Senelick (Austin: University of Texas Press, 1981), p. 111.

3. Vladimir Mayakovsky, *Pyesy* (Moscow: Detskaya literatura, 1971), p. 104.

4. Boris Zakhava, *Sovremenniki* (Moscow: Iskusstvo, 1969), p. 269–73.

5. *Vl. I. Nemirovich-Danchenko vedet repetitsiyu 'Tri sestry' A. P. Chekhova v postanovke MKhAT 1940 goda* (Moscow: Iskusstvo, 1963), pp. 149, 159, 189.

6. Michel St. Denis, *Theatre, the Rediscovery of Style* (New York: Theatre Arts Books, 1960), p. 53.

7. Quoted in *Newsnotes on Soviet & East European Drama & Theatre* III, 3 (Nov. 1983), pp. 2–3.

8. Jan McDonald, 'Production of Chekhov's plays in Britain before 1914,' *Theatre Notebook* 34, 1 (1980), pp. 25–36.

9. Quoted in *ibid.*

10. John Gielgud, *Stage Directions* (New York: Capricorn Books, 1966), p. 87.

11. *Ibid.*, p. 95.

12. *The New English Weekly* (18 June 1936), pp. 194–95.

13. Quoted in *Theatre Magazine* (New York, April 1938), p. 44.

14. *New Republic* (28 Dec. 1942), p. 858.

15. Private letter of Arthur Miller to the author, 6 May 1981.

16. Gordon Rogoff, 'Fire and Ice: Lee Strasberg,' *Tulane Drama Review* (Winter 1964), pp. 152–153.

17. 'Serban defends his "Cherry Orchard," ' *New York Times*

References

(13 Mar. 1977). See also Laurence Shyer, 'Andrei Serban directs Chekhov,' *Theater* (New Haven) (Fall/Winter 1981), pp. 56–65.

18. Peter Brook, *The Empty Space* (New York: Avon Books, 1969), p. 72.

19. Mel Gussow, 'Peter Brook returns to Chekhov's vision,' *New York Times* (19 Aug. 1981).

20. George Calderon, *Two Plays of Tchekhof* (London: Mitchell Kennerly, 1912), p. 8. For a fuller stage history of Chekhov's plays, see my essay 'Chekhov on Stage,' in *The Chekhov Handbook*, ed. Toby Clyman (Hamden, Conn.: Greenwood Press, 1985).

Bibliography

I. Works in Russian

Balukhaty, S. D., *Problema dramaticheskogo analiza: Chekhov.* (Leningrad: Academia, 1927. Reprint: Muenchen: Wilhelm Fink Verlag, 1969).

——————, and N. V. Petrov, *Dramaturgiya Chekhova.* (Kharkov: Izd. Kharkovskogo teatra russkoy dramy, 1935).

Berdnikov, G. P., *A. P. Chekhov: ideynye i tvorcheskie iskaniya.* (Moscow: Khudozhestvennaya literatura, 1970).

——————, *Chekhov-dramaturg: traditsii i novatorstvo v dramaturgii A. P. Chekhova.* (3rd ed. revised and enlarged. Moscow: Iskusstvo, 1972).

Brojde, Edgard, *Chekhov-myslitel, khudozhnik (100-letie tvorcheskogo puti). Katastrofa-vozrozhdenie.* (Frankfurt am Main: The author, 1980).

Bunin, I. A., *O Chekhove.* (New York: Chekhov Publishing House, 1955).

Chekhov, M. P., *Anton Chekhov i yego syuzhety* (Moscow: 9-e Ianvarya, 1923).

——————, *Anton Chekhov, teatr, aktery i 'Tatyana Repina'.* (Petrograd: Izd. avtora, 1924).

Anton Chekhov

——————, *Vokrug Chekhova. Vstrechi i vpechatleniya.* (Moscow: Moskovsky rabochy, 1980).

Efros, Nikolay, *'Tri sestri' i 'Vishnevy sad' v postanovke Moskovskom Khudozhestvennom teatra.* (Petrograd: Svetozar, 1919).

Gitovich, N. I., *Letopis zhizni i tvorchestva A. P. Chekhova.* (Moscow: Gos. Izd. Khudozhestvennoy literatury, 1955).

Gofman, Viktor, 'Yazyk i stil Chekhova-dramaturga,' in *Yazyk literatury.* (Leningrad: Khudozhestvennaya literatura, 1936).

Grigoryev, M., *Stsenicheskaya kompositsiya chekhovskikh pyes.* (Moscow: Izd. KUBS'a i V.L.Kh.I., 1924).

Lenin Library, Moscow, *Chekhovskie chteniya v Yalte. Chekhov i teatr.* (Moscow: Kniga, 1976).

Paperny, Z. S., *'Chayka' A. P. Chekhova.* (Moscow: Khudozhestvennaya literatura, 1980).

——————, *Zapisnye knizhki Chekhova.* (Moscow: Sovetsky pisatel, 1976).

——————, *Vopreki vsem pravilam: pyesy i vodevili Chekhova.* (Moscow: Iskusstvo, 1982).

Pokrovsky, V. I., ed. *Anton Pavlovich Chekhov. Yego zhizn i sochineniya.* (Moscow: Sklad v knizhnom magazina V. Spiridonova i A. Mikhailova, 1907).

Rudnitsky, K., 'Chekhov i rezhissery,' in *Voprosy teatra* 1 (Moscow 1965).

Shakh-Azizova, T. K., *Chekhov i zapadno-yevropeyskaya drama yego vremeni.* (Moscow: Nauka, 1966).

Skaftymov, A., 'O yedinstve formy i soderzhaniya v *Vishnevom sade*' and 'K voprosu o printsipakh postroeniya pyes A. P. Chekhova,' in *Nrastvennye iskaniya russkikh pisateley* (Moscow: Khudozhestvennaya literatura, 1972).

Sobolev, Yury, *Chekhov dramaturg* (Moscow: Federatsiya, 1930).

Stanislavsky, K. S., *A. P. Chekhov v Moskovskom Khudozhestvennom teatre,* ed. V. L. Vilenkin (Moscow: Izd. Muzeya MKhATa, 1947).

——————, *'Chayka' rezhisserskaya partitura.* (Leningrad–Moscow: Iskusstvo, 1938). Reprint: *Rezhisserskie ekzemplyary K. S. Stanislavskogo,* vol. 2. (Moscow: Iskusstvo, 1981).

——————, *Moya zhizn v iskusstve,* in *Sobranie sochineniya,* vol. 1 (Moscow: Iskusstvo, 1954).

Stroyeva, M. *Chekhov i Khudozhestvenny teatr.* (Moscow: Iskusstvo, 1955).

Bibliography

—————, Vl. I. Nemirovich-Danchenko vedet repetitsiyu. 'Tri sestry' A. P. Chekhova v postanovka MKhAT, 1940g. (Moscow: Iskusstvo, 1965).

Surkov, E. D., ed. Chekhov i teatr: pisma, feletony, sovremenniki o Chekhove-dramaturge (Moscow: Iskusstvo, 1961).

Yermilov, V., 'Chayka' materialy i issledovaniya. (Moscow: Iskusstvo, 1946).

—————, Dramaturgiya Chekhova. (Moscow: Sovetsky pisatel, 1948; enlarged ed., 1954).

Zingerman, B., 'Vodevili A. P. Chekhova,' Voprosy Teatra '72. (Moscow: Vserossiyskoe teatralnoe obshchestvo, 1973).

II. Works in Other Languages

Balukhaty, S., ed., The Seagull produced by Stanislavsky. Tr. D. Magarshack (London: Dennis Dobson, 1952).

Barricelli, Jean-Pierre, ed., Chekhov's great plays. A critical anthology (New York and London: New York University Press, 1981).

Bentley, Eric, 'Chekhov as a playwright,' Kenyon Review 2, 2 (Spring 1949): 227–50.

—————, 'Craftsmanship in Uncle Vanya,' in In Search of Theatre (New York: Vintage books, 1959).

Brahms, Caryl, Reflections in a Lake. A study of Chekhov's four greatest plays (London: Weidenfeld and Nicolson, 1976).

Bruford, W. H., Chekhov and his Russia: a sociological study. (London: Kegan Paul, Trench, Trubner, 1947).

'Chekhov Centenary Issue,' World Theatre 9, 2 (1960).

Chudakov, A. P., Chekhov's Poetics. Tr. F. J. Cruise and D. Dragt. (Ann Arbor: Ardis, 1983).

Clyman, Toby W., ed. A Chekhov Companion (Westport, Conn.: Greenwood Press, 1985).

Eekman, Thomas, ed. Anton Chekhov, 1860–1960. Some essays (Leyden: E. J. Brill, 1960).

————— and Paul Debreczeny, eds., Chekhov's art of writing. A collection of critical essays (Columbus, O.: Slavic Publishers, 1977).

Emeljanow, Victor, ed., Chekhov. The Critical Heritage (London: Routledge & Kegan Paul, 1981).

Anton Chekhov

Gottlieb, Vera, *Chekhov and the vaudeville. A study of Chekhov's one-act plays* (Cambridge: Cambridge University Press, 1982).

Hingley, Ronald, *Chekhov. A biographical and critical study.* Revised ed. (London: George Allen and Unwin, 1966).

—————, *A new life of Chekhov* (London: Oxford University Press, 1976).

Hristić, Jovan, *Le théâtre de Tchékhov.* Tr. Harita and Francis Wybrands (Lausanne: L'Age d'homme, 1982).

Jackson, Robert Louis, ed., *Chekhov. A collection of critical essays* (Englewood Cliffs, N.J.: Prentice-Hall, 1967).

Koteliansky, S. S., *Anton Tchekhov: Literary and theatrical reminiscences* (London: George Routledge and Sons, 1927).

Magarshack, David, *Chekhov the dramatist* (London: John Lehmann, 1952, reprint: London: Eyre Methuen, 1980).

—————, *The real Chekhov. An introduction to Chekhov's last plays* (London: George Allen and Unwin, 1972).

Moravčevich, Nicholas, 'Chekhov and naturalism: from affinity to divergence,' *Comparative Drama* 4 (Winter, 1970–71): 219–40.

—————, 'The obligatory scenes in Chekhov's dramas,' *Drama Critique* (Chicago) 9, 2 (Spring 1966): 97–104.

Nemirovich-Danchenko, Vladimir, *My Life in the Russian Theatre.* Tr. J. Cournos (London: Geoffrey Bles, 1937).

Peace, Richard, *Chekhov. A study of the four major plays* (New Haven and London: Yale University Press, 1983).

Pitcher, Harvey, *The Chekhov Play. A New Interpretation* (London: Chatto & Windus, 1973).

—————, *Chekhov's Leading Lady. A Portrait of the Actress Olga Knipper* (London: John Murray, 1979).

Raicu, John, 'Chekhov's use of church ritual in *Tatyana Repina*,' in *Themes in Drama 5*, ed. J. Redmond. (New York and London: Cambridge University Press, 1983).

Rayfield, Donald, *Chekhov. The Evolution of his art* (London: Elek, 1975).

Schmid, Herta, *Strukturalische Dramentheorie: semantische Analyse von Čechovs 'Ivanov' und 'Der Kirschgarten.'* (Kronberg: Scriptor Verlag, 1973).

Senelick, Laurence, 'Chekhov's response to Bernhardt,' in *Bernhardt and the Theatre of Her Time*, ed. E. Salmon (Westport, Conn.: Greenwood Press, 1984).

Bibliography

——————, 'The lake-shore of Bohemia: *The Seagull*'s theatrical context,' *Educational Theatre Journal* (May 1977): 199–213.

——————, ed. and tr. *Russian dramatic theory from Pushkin to the Symbolists* (Austin, Tex.: University of Texas Press, 1981).

Shevtsova, Maria, 'Chekhov in France, 1976–9: Productions by Strehler, Miquel and Pintilié,' in *Transformations in Modern European Drama*, ed. Ian Donaldson (Atlantic Highlands, N.J.: Humanities Press, 1983).

Silverstein, N. 'Chekhov's comic spirit and *The Cherry Orchard*,' *Modern Drama* 1, 2 (Sept. 1958): 91–100.

Simmons, Ernest, *Chekhov. A biography* (Boston: Little Brown, 1962).

Stanislavsky, K. S., *My Life in Art*, tr. J. J. Robbins (Boston: Little Brown, 1923).

Stroud, T., '*Hamlet* and *The Seagull*,' *Shakespeare Quarterly* 9, 3 (Summer, 1958): 367–72.

Styan, J. L., *Chekhov in Performance* (London: Cambridge University Press, 1972).

Valency, Maurice, *The Breaking string: the plays of Anton Chekhov* (New York: Oxford University Press, 1966).

Welleck, René and Nonna, D., eds., *Chekhov. New perspectives* (Englewood Cliffs, N.J.: Prentice-Hall, 1984).

Editions and Translations
of Chekhov

The authoritative edition of Chekhov's works in Russian is *Polnoe sobranie sochineny i pisem* (30 vols.), produced under the auspices of the Academy of Sciences of the USSR (Moscow, 1974–84). The plays with their variants, revisions and extensive notes are located in Volumes 11 to 13. In English, all of Chekhov's plays can readily be found in *The Oxford Chekhov*, translated and edited by Ronald Hingley, Vols. One to Three (London, 1964–83). This edition is especially useful for its translations of the variants and early drafts. Hingley, however, tries so hard to be idiomatically British, that he neglects Chekhov's careful repetitions of keywords and phrases.

Chekhov's plays have been regularly retranslated and adapted since the First World War. Some of the earliest English versions are the best: George Calderon's *Two Plays by Tchekhof* (London, 1912), not least for its excellent introduction, and Constance Garnett's *Nine Plays* (London, 1923), which, though old-fashioned, gives a sense of period gentility. Annotated editions of major works include *Chekhov's Plays*, ed. and trans. E. K. Bristow (New York, 1977); *The Cherry Orchard and The Seagull*, trans. Laurence Senelick (Arlington Heights, Ill., 1977) and *The*

Editions and Translations of Chekhov

Three Sisters, adapted by Randall Jarrell (New York, 1969). Other standard translations include those of Stark Young (New York, 1956), Ann Dunnigan (New York, 1964), and David Magarshack (London, 1968). (Magarshack has also translated an unabridged *Platonov*, London, 1964.)

Intelligent new versions include Michael Frayne's *The Cherry Orchard* (London, 1978) and *Three Sisters* (London, 1983), and *The Seagull* adapted by Thomas Kilroy (London, 1981) which sets it in turn-of-the-century Ireland. Less to be recommended are the versions of Elizaveta Fen, which cut lines and phrases without comment, and of Jean-Claude Van Itallie, which compound this fault by making all Chekhov's characters sound alike.

Useful editions of Chekhov's letters and notes include *The Notebooks of Anton Tchekhov, together with Reminiscences of Tchekhov by Maxim Gorky*, tr. S. S. Koteliansky and Leonard Woolf (Richmond, 1921); *Letters on the short story, the drama and other literary topics*, ed. Louis S. Friedland (London, 1924; repr. New York, 1966); *Letters of Anton Chekhov*, ed. Simon Karlinsky, tr. Michael Heim (London and New York, 1973); and *The Letters of Anton Chekhov*, ed. Avrahm Yarmolinsky (New York, 1973).

Index

Index

Index

Index

Index

Index

Index

Index